the Forerunners

Mark E. Petersen

Bookcraft
Salt Lake City, Utah

Library of Congress Catalog Card Number: 79-53831
ISBN O-88494-376-3

2nd Printing, 1980

Lithographed in the United States of America
PUBLISHERS PRESS
Salt Lake City, Utah

Contents

"And thou, child, shalt be called the prophet of the Highest: for thou shalt go before the face of the Lord to prepare his ways;

"To give knowledge of salvation unto his people by the remission of their sins,

"Through the tender mercy of our God; whereby the dayspring from on high hath visited us,

"To give light to them that sit in darkness and in the shadow of death, to guide our feet into the way of peace.

"And the child grew, and waxed strong in spirit, and was in the deserts till the day of his shewing unto Israel." (Luke 1:76-80.)

And his name was John.

"Wherefore, I the Lord, knowing the calamity which should come upon the inhabitants of the earth, called upon my servant Joseph Smith, Jun., and spake unto him from heaven, and gave him commandments;

"And also gave commandments to others, that they should proclaim these things unto the world; and all this that it might be fulfilled, which was written by the prophets—"   (D&C 1:17-18.)

PART ONE

THE PREPARATION FOR THE LORD'S BIRTH

One

The Lord's Messengers

Since the Creation the most significant messages ever given to mankind were those proclaiming the coming to earth of the Lord Jesus Christ.

Through the ages the prophets have spoken of two such advents, one in the meridian of time when he would take upon himself mortality and accomplish the Atonement; the other his glorious second coming which will usher in his millennial reign.

For each advent a prophetic messenger was assigned to go before him and prepare the way. One was John the Baptist, of whom Jesus said there was no greater prophet born of woman. (See Luke 7:28.) The other was Joseph Smith, Jr., designated in modern scripture as having done more for the salvation of mankind than anyone else on earth, with the sole exception of our Redeemer, the Lord Jesus Christ himself. (See D&C 135.)

Both advents had been foretold by the prophets through the ages. The people were amply forewarned concerning the Lord's first coming; for as Peter told Cornelius the Gentile:

"To him give all the prophets witness, that through his name whosoever believeth in him shall receive remission of sins." (Acts 10:43.)

When Paul was in Rome "there came many to him into his lodging; to whom he expounded and testified the kingdom of God, persuading them concerning Jesus, both out of the law of Moses, and out of the prophets from morning till evening." (Acts 28:23.) This scripture indicates that the prophets who lived long before Paul had written of Christ.

When this same apostle wrote to the Romans, he also affirmed that Christ had been "promised afore by his prophets in the holy scriptures." (Romans 1:2.)

Jesus himself taught that Moses wrote of His coming, and said:

"For had ye believed Moses, ye would have believed me: for he wrote of me. But if ye believe not his writings, how shall ye believe my words?" (John 5:46-47.)

As the resurrected Lord walked on the way to Emmaus, he taught these facts to the disciples who accompanied him:

"O fools, and slow of heart to believe all that the prophets have spoken:

"Ought not Christ to have suffered these things, and to enter into his glory?

"And beginning at Moses and all the prophets, he expounded unto them in all the scriptures the things concerning himself." (Luke 24:25-27.)

Among the best remembered passages from the Old Testament predicting the coming of the Lord in the flesh are those from Isaiah. There is the familiar: "Therefore the Lord himself shall give you a sign; Behold, a virgin shall conceive, and bear a son, and shall call his name Immanuel." (Isaiah 7:14.)

Isaiah wrote in prophecy concerning the Christ in these beloved words:

"For unto us a child is born, unto us a son is given: and the government shall be upon his shoulder: and his name shall be called Wonderful, Counsellor, The mighty God, The everlasting Father, The Prince of Peace." (Isaiah 9:6.)

And who can ever forget Isaiah's fifty-third chapter, one of the most beautiful expressions in all holy writ? The entire chapter should be read with reverence and care, but let us review a part of it:

"He is despised and rejected of men; a man of sorrows, and acquainted with grief: and we hid as it were our faces from him; he was despised, and we esteemed him not.

"Surely he hath borne our griefs, and carried our sorrows: yet we did esteem him stricken, smitten of God, and afflicted.

"But he was wounded for our transgressions, he was bruised for our iniquities: the chastisement of our peace was upon him; and with his stripes we are healed.

"All we like sheep have gone astray; we have turned every one to his own way; and the Lord hath laid on him the iniquity of us all.

"He was oppressed, and he was afflicted, yet he opened not his mouth: he is brought as a lamb to the slaughter, and as a sheep before her shearers is dumb, so he openeth not his mouth. . . .

"And he made his grave with the wicked, and with the rich in his death. . . . he bare the sin of many, and made intercession for the transgressors." (Isaiah 53:3-12.)

Words could hardly portray more clearly the mission and the atonement of the Christ; surely Isaiah was greatly inspired as he penned those passages. No wonder the Lord told the Nephites:

"And now, behold, I say unto you, that ye ought to search these things. Yea, a commandment I give unto you that ye search these things diligently; for great are the words of Isaiah.

"For surely he spake as touching all things concerning my people which are of the house of Israel; therefore it must needs be that he must speak also to the Gentiles.

"And all things that he spake have been and shall be, even according to the words which he spake." (3 Nephi 23:1-3.)

Centuries before the birth of the Savior, Book of Mormon prophets portrayed his coming in great detail. This was reaffirmed by the Savior himself, who referred to prophets on both hemispheres. Said he to the Nephites:

"Behold, I am he of whom Moses spake, saying: A prophet shall the Lord your God raise up unto you of your brethren, . . ."

And then the Lord said:

"Verily I say unto you, yea, and all the prophets from Samuel and those that follow after, as many as have spoken, have testified of me." (3 Nephi 20:23-24.)

The Prophet Jacob, who lived more than five hundred years before the birth of the Savior, wrote: "Behold, I say unto you that none of the prophets have written, nor prophesied, save they have spoken concerning this Christ." (Jacob 7:11.)

Jacob also taught directly: "Wherefore, as I said unto you, it must needs be expedient that Christ—for in the last night the angel spake unto me that this should be his name—should come among the Jews, . . ." (2 Nephi 10:3.)

The ancient prophets Zenos and Zenock, quoted in the Book of Mormon, testified that Christ should come, that he would be crucified and would come forth in resurrection. They spoke of the destruction which would take place at the time of the Crucifixion, and bore strong testimony that Jesus would be born the Son of Almighty God. (See 1 Nephi 19:1-16.)

It is not known when those two prophets lived nor where they labored, but Nephi quoted them in his record nearly six hundred years before the birth of the Savior.

The vision of the first Nephi is one of the most dramatic, most moving revelations of the coming of Christ on record, and this vision also was written soon after six hundred B.C. (See 1 Nephi 10, 11, 12, 13.)

Nephi called him the Messiah and the Savior and told of his baptism by John in Bethabara. He saw the Savior in vision, saw the Crucifixion, was shown the mother of the Savior, the most beautiful of women, and was told by the Being who stood by him, "Ye shall bear record that it is the Son of God." (1 Nephi 11:7.)

Nephi saw that the Savior would choose twelve special witnesses, known as the twelve disciples of the Lamb of God (See 1 Nephi 12:7-10), and testified that Jesus of Nazareth was to be "the Messiah who is the Lamb of God, of whom the Holy Ghost beareth record, from the beginning of the world until this time, and from this time henceforth and forever." (1 Nephi 12:18.)

Many other references both in ancient and modern scriptures might be reproduced to show that "all the prophets gave witness" unto him and his coming.

These references speak both of his first coming in mortality and of his final coming in great glory when he comes to judgment, when he will be seen in the midst of the skies and will descend with "ten thousand of his Saints"; when there will be a resurrection of the just, when wickedness will be destroyed; when he will come to the Mount of Olives, and there be recognized by the besieged Jews; when he will identify himself to them and say as he is asked about the wounds in his hands and feet that they are "those with which I was wounded in the house of my friends." (See Zechariah 13:6; 14:1-21; D&C 45:51-53.)

Job cried out and said: "For I know that my redeemer liveth, and that he shall stand at the latter day upon the earth;

"And though after my skin worms destroy my body, yet in my flesh shall I see God." (Job 19:25-26.)

Christ is spoken of in the Psalms: "Our God shall come, and shall not keep silence: a fire shall devour before him, and it shall be very tempestuous round about him;

"He shall call to the heavens from above, and to the earth, that he may judge his people." (Psalms 50:3-4.)

Isaiah spoke of the Savior's second coming in judgment "with a recompense." (See Isaiah 35:4.) Joel spoke of the sun and moon being darkened before His coming, and he added, "and the stars shall withdraw their shining." (See Joel 3:15.)

Zechariah told of the Armageddon which should precede His coming to Jerusalem in that fateful period when all nations shall be gathered there to battle: "Then shall the Lord go forth, and fight against those nations . . . and his feet shall stand in that day upon the mount of Olives." The Mount shall cleave in twain, and the Jews shall rush into the ravine thus formed and meet him there, face to face. (Zechariah 14; Ezekiel 38, 39; D&C 45.)

Malachi was not silent about this important event either, and he declared: "Who may abide the day of his coming? and who shall stand when he appeareth? for he is like a refiner's fire and like fullers' soap." The day that comes shall burn the wicked, who shall be as stubble. (See Malachi 3, 4.)

The Savior, of course, foretold his own second coming, as we have it recorded in the twenty-fourth chapter of Matthew, with fearsome details being given. But he included the prediction that before the Second Coming, the gospel of the kingdom would be preached to all the world as a witness to all nations, and then the end would come.

The two advents of the Lord are to be in great contrast. His first coming was as the humble Lamb of God, also as the Good Shepherd. He was despised and persecuted and finally killed. Few accepted him.

But his second coming will be so spectacular, so world-shaking and extensive that all men shall see it together.

For each advent, however, a forerunner was chosen to prepare the way. Each coming would require its own particular kind of advance preparation. Hence, each was given its own forerunner, specially chosen for the work.

John the Baptist prepared the way for the first coming. Joseph Smith, Jr., was the forerunner for the second, and his work has been and is now being sustained and furthered by each succeeding prophet called to lead the Church.

This will continue until Christ himself shall come as King of Kings and Lord of Lords to reign on the earth with his Saints for a thousand years.

Two

Making His Way Ready

Advance preparation for the Lord's coming was vital both in the meridian of time and in the latter days.

In all fairness, a just and ample opportunity was planned for mankind to prepare for these great events. The people must be warned of the impending fulfillment of prophecy; for if they would humbly believe the warning, they would be given some understanding of the significance of what was soon to take place.

When the Savior came as a mortal Being he was met by a hostile world ready to attack, humiliate, and even kill him at any moment. But there were friends who took his part and believed his words and followed him. Who were they? Where did they come from?

An advance messenger had provided those friends. He had preached repentance to the people before Christ's ministry began and had baptized those who believed his words. He especially had spoken of One greater than himself who would come after him, baptizing with fire and the Holy Ghost.

By telling his followers of the Christ who soon would

come, this advance messenger built into their minds a keen sense of expectancy which made it easy for them to receive the Lord when he did appear.

Without such faithful friends to whom the Christ could readily turn, his difficult mission would have been much harder indeed. It was the plan of God that those who believed the teachings of John the Baptist, his advance messenger, also would recognize the voice of the Good Shepherd when they heard it and follow him. From among such friends and believers, the Savior could well choose righteous and already converted men to assist him in gathering his flock. They could become the faithful and devout nucleus of his kingdom as he established it in his day. They would be able then to carry on the work following the passion and ascension of the Lord.

All of this depended on the prior labors of John the Baptist, that specially chosen minister sent to prepare the way. For as the Apostle Paul said, how could they believe on One of whom they had not heard; and how could they hear without a preacher, and how could this preacher accomplish such a work without a divine call? (See Romans 10:14-15; Hebrews 5:4.)

The Lord's first coming was a humble one indeed, hence the small-scale, low-key preparation which was limited to an area of but a few square miles.

John's preaching began as the voice of one crying in the wilderness. The curious came out to see him, for he was thought to be like a "wild man." Some soldiers came evidently to guard against violence, and John preached to them, too.

A few people were converted and baptized. Others, such as the scribes and elders, challenged him. Who was this new preacher? What right did he have to stir up the people? Why had he come, anyway?

Some of his less prejudiced hearers were puzzled by his message. Others wondered if he were the Messiah, for there was an air of expectancy among the people.

All that John accomplished was prologue. He himself was filled with a strong sense of anticipation, for he knew and had been told by the One who sent him that the Son of God would come in that very day, and that he, John, was His advance messenger.

When the Savior came for baptism, the looked-for sign was given. The voice came from heaven and the dove descended. From above, God issued the declaration, "This is my beloved Son"; and from John came the word to his own little flock, "Behold, the Lamb of God." Jesus was fully identified.

The Baptist explained that this Personage who now had come was indeed the expected One whose shoelaces he felt unworthy to tie. It was He who would baptize with fire and the Holy Ghost.

The appearance and baptism of Jesus seem to have taken place in a fairly remote place. But crowds came out to learn from John, who was clad in rough clothes, who had not enjoyed the culture of the city, and who was unknown to the respected scribes, chief priests, and elders.

Simple as was the ministry of the Baptist, it was nevertheless in keeping with the work of the King of Kings who came after him and descended below all things in coming into mortality and was even born in a stable. Jesus' humble birth harmonized also with the rest of his mission, for he walked the dusty roads of Palestine, went hungry, and grew tired. He was despised and rejected of men, a man of sorrows and acquainted with grief. His ministry eventually led to condemnation in Pilate's judgment hall and then to the cross on Calvary between two thieves.

But the Second Coming will have none of that. It will be in tremendous contrast to the first advent. It will be a time of divine judgment—destruction for the wicked and reward for the righteous.

All mankind will see it together, for the heavens will roll back like a scroll and the Redeemer will appear in glory, accompanied by thousands of his Saints. Stars will fall, the sun will hide its face, and the moon will turn red as blood.

For such an event the preparation must be as extensive in proportion as the coming itself; therefore, the work projected by the Lord as a preface to his climactic appearance is vast indeed. It will require continued prophetic leadership and the labors of millions of people over a period of years.

For example, the Lord in that day will suddenly come to his temple. (See Malachi 3:1.) Therefore a temple must be built, not such as the world builds, but his kind of temple. But who can the builder be? Who can know how to plan and build to meet the needs? Where will it be located, and what will be its ultimate purpose?

One of the great steps in preparing for the Lord's latter-day coming must be to turn the hearts of the children to their fathers, and of the fathers to the children. What does this mean? How can that be accomplished and by whom? Who can turn such a key? And yet if it were not done, the whole earth would be smitten with a curse. (See Malachi 4:6.)

A sacred book was destined to be given to the world in a miraculous way. By act of God it would come as a message to modern mankind from an ancient people who had been destroyed suddenly. It would "speak out of the ground," and its message would be "low out of the dust." Who would bring it forth, and to whom would it be given by some miraculous means? What modern person would read its ancient and unknown text? The words of the book would be given to a learned man to be read, but his worldly knowledge would prove inadequate. The scripture says that the book itself would be given to an unlearned man who then would publish it, and it would be a marvelous work and a wonder. (See Isaiah 29; Ezekiel 37: 15-22.)

What of this book? Has it appeared? If so, who was its author, translator, and publisher? Is it being distributed abroad now as part of the gospel which was to be taken to all nations, or is it some hidden volume having a limited circulation only? What was its purpose? If it has not yet appeared, what may we now expect in the future?

But even all of this is not the full extent of the advance preparation for the Lord. There is more, much more.

A body of the Lord's Saints was destined to assemble in the tops of the mountains, in a place exalted above the hills, where they would build the Lord's temple. To this place people from "all nations" would flow. Has this prophecy been fulfilled? If not, what may we expect of the future in this regard? (See Isaiah 2:2-3; Micah 4:1-2.)

It is declared in scripture that a remnant of the Jews will

return to Palestine before the coming of the Savior, for he will meet them there in a time of war and show them the marks of the Crucifixion. Then will they be converted and acknowledge him as their Messiah. What will lead up to such an event? (See Zechariah 12-14; Ezekiel 38, 39; D&C 45.)

A new and latter-day dispensation of the gospel was promised, to be given as a witness to all nations, following which "shall the end come." (See Matthew 24.) But who was—or is—or shall be—capable of receiving the gospel and have power to dispense it to all mankind? What preachers will be required to assist in such an international project? Who will have authority to call them and ordain them to the work?

How would this dispensation originate? Was it really needed, this new "bringing forth" of the gospel? Was not the truth already on earth? If so, why the necessity of a re-dissemination of God's word?

Is the new dispensation in and of itself evidence that the gospel as at first given to mankind was lost, thus making a restoration necessary?

Scripture tells us repeatedly about a new dissemination or restoration of the truth and explains further that it will be accomplished through the coming of an angel from heaven. He is to bear this everlasting gospel (and there is only one) to earth so that it can be taken to every nation, kindred, tongue, and people.

When was this angel to come? Was there a predetermined time? One is mentioned in the scriptural prediction. It was to be in the "hour of God's judgment." (See Revelation 14:6-7.)

To whom would he deliver his precious message? Would it be to some prominent world figure commanding international attention or to some obscure person, such as John the Baptist was in his day? John was the forerunner for the Lord's first coming. Would this modern prophet be his counterpart?

Let us remember that this angel, of necessity, would have to come to some prophet of God living on the earth in order to preserve the integrity of the words of Amos: "Surely the Lord God will do nothing, but he revealeth his secret unto his servants the prophets." (Amos 3:7.)

Who would this prophet be? Most churches reject the idea of modern prophets. Then would there be such a man on earth to receive this angel? And if not, what could God do to fulfill his prophecy—raise up a new one?

But even more preparation was predicted.

"A nation would be born in a day" among the modern descendants of Joseph who was sold into Egypt. This remarkable and surprising occurrence would be a major development of this new dispensation of the gospel and would be directly related to the sacred volume which would "speak low out of the dust." How can all this be?

As has been said, a remnant of Jews will return to Palestine as part of this latter-day preparation. They will rebuild the old city of Jerusalem. (See Jeremiah 16:14-16; 23:2-8; 33:7-11; Amos 9:14-15; D&C 45.)

But another and different people will build a second holy city—the New Jerusalem—in the heartland of the United States of America, and from it the word and law of the Lord will go forth. (See Isaiah 2; Micah 4; D&C 42:9, 67; 45:66; 48:5; 84:2; 133:56; 3 Nephi 20:22, 21:23; Ether 13:4-11.)

Who will build this holy city? Where will it be located? Who can know? When will it be done? God knows. Only he can direct the work. But that will require revelation, and he works only through his prophets. Where will we find such men?

Since the Lord works only through prophets (Amos 3:7), then all of these extensive preparations for Jesus' second coming must be directed through some heaven-chosen seer. But has the prophet come already? Some of this preparatory work has been accomplished, such as the return of nearly three million Jews to Palestine. That is certainly one of the signs of the times—a sign to the world that God is now fulfilling his predictions. Has the prophet come already, or do we wait for some future messenger?

Such a forerunner, of necessity, must have a calling like that of John the Baptist and be a literal preparer of the way of the Master. But unlike the simple work of John, this modern prophet's assignment will be on a vast scale, even of worldwide proportions, for the decreed work is that broad.

Only one of God's most talented and faithful sons, chosen as was Jeremiah (See Jeremiah 1:5) before he was born, could fill the measure of so great a calling. And such a one was chosen indeed. He was Joseph Smith, Jr., the American prophet.

As John the Baptist was the promised messenger of old, Joseph Smith was the promised modern messenger of the covenant. (See Malachi 3:1.)

Both he and John went before the Lord in their own times preparing his way. Both closed their missions in martyrdom.

Three

The Premise of Amos

The premise laid down by Amos the prophet is basic to all of God's dealings with the human race. It is a simple one: The Almighty ministers to mankind only through the agency of his living prophets who in turn receive their guidance by divine revelation.

His inspired words were:

"Surely the Lord God will do nothing, but he revealeth his secret unto his servants the prophets." (Amos 3:7.)

This is the unchanging, overall basis of God's relationship with men. Should anyone doubt the wording in the King James translation, this doctrine may be amply sustained through modern translations of the Bible.

For example, the Jewish Publication Society of America, headquartered in Philadelphia, produced a modern version of the Old Testament according to the Masoretic text, in which the Amos passage is given as follows:

"For the Lord God will do nothing, But He revealeth His counsel unto His servants the prophets."

The Roman Catholic Jerusalem Bible renders it:

"No more does the Lord Yahveh do anything without revealing his plans to his servants the prophets."

Another Catholic translation, produced in England in 1954, by Monsignor Knox under the authority of Bernardus Cardinal Griffin reads:

"Never does he act, but his servants the prophets are in the secret."

The American Translation by Smith and Goodspeed says:

"Surely he will do nothing, the Lord God, except he reveal his purpose to his servants the prophets."

The Moffatt translation reads: "The Lord Eternal never does anything without telling his servants the prophets."

Other modern translations similarly set forth this doctrine with complete clarity. It is beyond ambiguity or misunderstanding.

The Savior also emphasized this pattern while he was on earth. Teaching that his work was based on revelation, he sent the Holy Ghost to provide that revelation after his ascension. (See John 14:15-25; Acts 2:1-18.)

When he asked his disciples who people thought he was, and they replied that some thought he was John the Baptist come back to life, Jeremiah, Elias, or some other prophet returned to earth, he asked directly: "Whom say ye that I am?"

Peter gave the answer: "Thou art the Christ, the Son of the living God."

In reply the Savior confirmed Amos's doctrine of revelation and said that flesh and blood had not revealed this testimony to Peter; for God, the Eternal Father, had done so. And he said further, referring to this principle of revelation from God to man, "upon this rock [principle] I will build my church; and the gates of hell shall not prevail against it." (Matthew 16:13-18.)

Since he would build his Church upon the principle of revelation, it was obvious that he would direct his people over the years by that means. Hence, living apostles and prophets were placed in the Church to receive those revelations. (See Ephesians 4:11-14.)

He could not direct his Church without speaking to it. It

required guidance that was understandable and direct. Mortal men could not know the will of God unless it was revealed to them.

If God will do nothing except he shall work through prophets, as Amos said, He certainly would not run his Church without them. Therefore, they were placed in it "for the perfecting of the saints, for the work of the ministry, for the edifying of the body of Christ." (Ephesians 4:12.)

It goes without saying that it is through prophets that God gives revelation, and he thus controls his purposes among men. But it is equally clear that without such revelation to the prophets "the Lord God will do *nothing.*"

Surely this great principle would apply to the two most important spiritual events in all history—that of the coming of the mortal Savior and the accomplishment of his atonement. Of course, Christians agree that it did; and they accept John as the Lord's mortal forerunner. But since His second coming will be world-shattering, would not the principle of prophetic ministration apply there, too?

Since the passage in Matthew (16:13-19) has been subject to wide discussion over the meaning of the Savior's words, it may be well to glance for a moment at some modern renderings of those verses. It is interesting that they clearly sustain the basic premise of Amos.

Dr. Hugh J. Schonfield, noted Jewish scholar, in his Authentic New Testament gives this rendering:

"Simon Peter answered, You are the Messiah, the Son of the living God.

"How fortunate you are, impulsive Simon, Jesus said to him. No mortal disclosed this to you: it was my Father. And so I tell you, since you are Peter, upon that rock I will found my community, and the gates of hell shall not prevail against it." (page 67.) Obviously he was speaking of revelation.

A recent Catholic version gives essentially the same meaning:

"Then Simon Peter answered, Thou art the Christ, the Son of the living God. And Jesus answered him, Blessed art thou, Simon, son of Jona, for it is not flesh and blood, it is my Father in heaven, that has revealed this to thee, and I tell thee in my turn, that thou art Peter, and it is upon this rock that I will build my Church." (Knox version.) It is clear that Peter was not the "rock," but revelation was.

The Jerusalem Bible, also a Catholic version, reads in part:

"Simon, son of Jonah, you are a happy man! Because it is not flesh and blood that revealed this to you but my Father in heaven. So now I say to you: You are Peter and on this rock I will build my Church." Again, the subject was revelation.

The scriptures here show that Peter declared Jesus to be the Christ. Jesus in turn declared that Simon was Peter. Each in turn gave the name of the other.

Then the Lord spoke of communication, the manner in which Peter learned of Christ's identity. It was on this principle of divine communication—in other words, revelation—that the Lord would build his Church.

When William Barclay of the Church of Scotland prepared his translation of the New Testament, he commented on this passage from Matthew in his *Daily Study of the Bible*:

"The rock is the truth that Jesus Christ is the Son of the living God. To Peter that great truth had been divinely revealed. It was God Himself who had opened Peter's eyes to that great discovery. The fact that Jesus Christ is the Son of God is indeed the foundation stone of the Church's faith and belief. On that great truth the Church is founded for ever and ever. This explanation holds that the *divinely revealed truth that Jesus is the Son of God is the only foundation on which the Church is founded.*" (Volume 2, The Gospel of Matthew, pages 154-155. Italics added.)

It is clear then, from the various versions of the scripture, that the testimony was given to Peter by divine revelation, which is basic in the Church, and that Jesus was talking to Peter about revelation, which was the means by which he obtained his testimony.

The Apostle Paul in his writings indicated that everyone may know—also by revelation—that Jesus is the Christ, for this testimony is borne to the believers by the power of the Holy Ghost. (See 1 Corinthians 12:3.)

The Holy Ghost is a revelator. That is one of his great functions. (See John 16:13.) So again it is made clear that God's dealings with mankind are channeled by the power of revelation to prophets without whom, as Amos said, "the Lord God will do nothing."

The testimony of Jesus is basic to the success of a Christian life. Without that testimony one cannot claim a true conversion to Christ. Our whole religion rests upon him, for there is no salvation in any other name, as Peter declared so emphatically. (See Acts 4:12.)

The atonement of Christ, upon which our salvation depends, is the most important event that has ever happened on earth.

Since God will do nothing except he revealeth his secret unto his servants the prophets, most assuredly he never would have sent his Beloved Son into the world to work out his ultimate atonement without the accompanying ministry of divinely called prophets.

But let us ask this: Could there be any preparation for the coming of Christ if the sacredness and significance of the *name of Christ* were not proclaimed?

It is conversion to that name, it is acceptance of that Christ, it is the desire to benefit from his atonement which brings about the development of the "broken heart and contrite spirit," without which no one may truly come to him.

John the Baptist courageously declared the name and lofty position of the Savior as the Lamb of God.

Joseph Smith to his death affirmed the divinity of Jesus of Nazareth, and declared him to be the literal and physical son of the Almighty Father of heaven and earth.

No matter how many people John may have gathered about him because of his personality and courage; no matter how many millions may respond to the message of the Prophet Joseph Smith, if a person lacks the testimony of Christ any such response would be meaningless and valueless. The *testimony of Jesus burning in the hearts of humble converts to the truth* is the real preparation for Christ's coming.

Thus, he will come to those converts who love him, worship him, and willingly place their all on the altar to bring about his purposes. It will be they who will build the New Jerusalem, establish Zion in the tops of the mountains, bring forth the book from "low out of the dust," and take the everlasting gospel to every nation, kindred, tongue, and people as a final warning before the end comes.

Hence, the great necessity of the forerunners John and Joseph. Hence, the divinity of their calls. Hence, the significance of their divinely revealed testimonies.

It is conversion to Christ that prepares the way of Christ. Nothing else will do.

And how is the testimony of Jesus related to prophecy? "The testimony of Jesus is the spirit of prophecy" (Revelation 19:10), and "no man can say that Jesus is the Lord, but by the Holy Ghost." (1 Corinthians 12:3.)

Four

The Stamp of Divinity

Before Christ was born, John the Baptist was ushered into this mortal life. Before Jesus began his ministry, John was already teaching, baptizing, and bearing testimony of the forthcoming Messiah.

John's work bore the unmistakable stamp of divinity. He was raised up to this work by act of God (see D&C 84:27) and was acknowledged (even before his conception) as the forerunner of the Savior by the Angel Gabriel. (See Luke 1:17.)

Was it not significant that the same angelic messenger should make the announcement of the coming of both John and Jesus, thus associating their ministries from the very beginning?

The angel's words to Zacharias, John's father, were startling and revealing. Note the angelic predictions:

"Many shall rejoice at his birth."

"He shall be great in the sight of the Lord."

"He shall be filled with the Holy Ghost, even from his mother's womb."

"Many of the children of Israel shall he turn to the Lord their God."

"He shall go before him in the spirit and power of Elias."

"To make ready a people prepared for the Lord." (Luke 1: 14-17.)

The prophecy made by Zacharias concerning his son is also most revealing:

"Thou, child, shalt be called the prophet of the Highest."

"Thou shalt go before the face of the Lord to prepare his ways."

"To give knowledge of salvation unto this people by the remission of their sins, through the tender mercy of our God."

"To give light to them that sit in darkness and in the shadow of death."

"To guide our feet into the way of peace." (Luke 1:76-79.)

To what other prophet since the days of Adam was such a mission given? To none, of course, not even to Moses!

Many fail to realize that John was a preacher of the gospel of Jesus Christ inasmuch as he declared the Savior's name and that in such a calling John was able to fulfill these predictions.

He was great in the sight of the Lord. He did turn many of the children of Israel to the Lord their God; and the manner in which he did so was that he taught his followers concerning Jesus, and when the Lord appeared he directed them to hearken to Jesus.

That is the manner in which he made "ready a people prepared for the Lord." It was for this purpose that he went "before the face of the Lord to prepare his way."

By his faithful preaching and by directing his followers to accept the Savior, he did "give them knowledge of salvation." He did "give light to them that sat in darkness."

Since Jesus was the Prince of Peace, it was abundantly true that John, directing his own followers toward Christ, did guide their feet into the way of peace.

As we are told in the Doctrine and Covenants, John was raised up by act of God and was "filled with the Holy Ghost from his mother's womb." He was "baptized when he was yet in his childhood and was ordained by the angel of God at the time he was eight days old unto this power, to overthrow the kingdom of the Jews, and to make straight the way of the Lord before the face of his people, to prepare them for the coming of the Lord, in whose hand is given all power." (D&C 84:27-28.)

Note the significance of those words. When John was only eight days old he was ordained:

1.   To overthrow the kingdom of the Jews. Because of their wicked reaction to the teachings of both John and Jesus, Jewry was crushed shortly after their death.

2.   To make straight the way of the Lord before the face of the people. This he did by not only calling them to repentance, but also by preaching "straight" doctrine and correct gospel truths in the face of a host of man-made creeds and traditions. Those who accepted John were indeed "set straight" in that day of religious confusion.

3.   To prepare the people for the coming of the Lord. As a matter of fact, *John the Baptist opened the door to the Christian era for all time to come*. Therefore, he was one of the most important persons who ever lived on earth. It is no wonder that the Savior said no greater prophet had ever been born of woman. (See Luke 7:28.)

True, the Christian dispensation dates directly to the coming of Jesus himself, but John opened the door for him, and thus ushered in that great era. It was John who introduced Christ to the world when He came; it was John who fully identified him, called him the Lamb of God, and declared Jesus to be the One to baptize with fire and the Holy Ghost.

John's converts, of necessity, were converts to Christ even before Jesus began his ministry, for John preached of Christ. Those were the people prepared for their Lord by means of conversion by John. They had listened to John testify of the One who was greater than himself and who would shortly come. They looked forward to the Lord, and when he came they accepted and followed him. This was the preparation accomplished by John.

It is interesting to note the harmony between the ancient and modern scriptures as they speak of John. In both writings we read that:

He was to make straight the way of the Lord.

He was to give knowledge of salvation to people who sat in

darkness, through declaring the coming of Christ and by administering baptism for the remission of sins.

He was to prepare the people for the coming of the Lord, or, to use the biblical expression, "make ready a people prepared for the Lord."

It should be remembered that he prepared the people for the Lord by preaching to them about the Lord, testifying that He was their Savior, their Redeemer, the literal Lamb of God.

John had thus prepared a congregation of believers for the Savior from whom the Lord could call his leaders and among whom he could establish the nucleus of his kingdom.

Jesus did not call his disciples from among total strangers. He obviously called them from among John's believers who already had fully accepted the Savior because John had taught them so.

John was vigorous in his preaching. The scripture reads:

"And he came into all the country about Jordan, preaching the baptism of repentance for the remission of sins;

"As it is written in the book of the words of Esaias the prophet, saying, The voice of one crying in the wilderness, Prepare ye the way of the Lord, make his paths straight.

"Every valley shall be filled, and every mountain and hill shall be brought low; and the crooked shall be made straight, and the rough ways shall be made smooth;

"And all flesh shall see the salvation of God.

"Then said he to the multitude that came forth to be baptized of him, O generation of vipers, who hath warned you to flee from the wrath to come?

"Bring forth therefore fruits worthy of repentance, and begin not to say within yourselves, We have Abraham to our father: for I say unto you, That God is able of these stones to raise up children unto Abraham.

"And now also the axe is laid unto the root of the trees: every tree therefore which bringeth not forth good fruit is hewn down, and cast into the fire.

"And the people asked him, saying, What shall we do then?

"He answereth and saith unto them, He that hath two coats, let him impart to him that hath none; and he that hath meat, let him do likewise.

"Then came also publicans to be baptized, and said unto him, Master, what shall we do?

"And he said unto them, Exact no more than that which is appointed you.

"And the soldiers likewise demanded of him, saying, And what shall we do? And he said unto them, Do violence to no man, neither accuse any falsely; and be content with your wages." (Luke 3:3-14.)

The people wondered about John's identity. They were full of expectation concerning the coming of the Messiah, and some wondered if John were the Lord, a thing which he stoutly denied, saying:

"I indeed baptize you with water; but one mightier than I cometh, the latchet of whose shoes I am not worthy to unloose: he shall baptize you with the Holy Ghost and with fire:

"Whose fan is in his hand, and he will throughly purge his floor, and will gather the wheat into his garner; but the chaff he will burn with fire unquenchable.

"And many other things in his exhortation preached he unto the people." (Luke 3:16-18.)

When the Prophet Joseph Smith translated Luke, he amended these passages as follows:

"The voice of one crying in the wilderness, Prepare ye the way of the Lord, and make his paths straight.

"For behold, and lo, he shall come, as it is written in the book of the prophets, to take away the sins of the world, and to bring salvation unto the heathen nations, to gather together those who are lost, who are of the sheepfold of Israel;

"Yea, even the dispersed and afflicted; and also to prepare the way, and make possible the preaching of the gospel unto the Gentiles;

"And to be a light unto all who sit in darkness, unto the uttermost parts of the earth; to bring to pass the resurrection from the dead, and to ascend up on high, to dwell on the right hand of the Father.

"Until the fulness of time, and the law and the testimony shall be sealed, and the keys of the kingdom shall be delivered up again unto the Father;

"To administer justice unto all; to come down in judgment upon all, and to convince all the ungodly of their ungodly deeds, which they have committed; and all this in the day that he shall come;

"For it is a day of power; yea, every valley shall be filled, and every mountain and hill shall be brought low; the crooked shall be made straight, and the rough ways made smooth;

"And all flesh shall see the salvation of God." (Inspired Version, Luke 3:4-11.)

Matthew records that "John had his raiment of camel's hair, and a leathern girdle about his loins; and his meat was locusts and wild honey." (Matthew 3:4.)

Bible dictionaries indicate that locusts were ceremonially clean under the law of Moses. (See Leviticus 11:22.) "The fleshy portion was roasted and eaten, and was the food of many people. Among the poor of Palestine today, locusts are still eaten as a basic food. The locusts have antennae shorter than that of grasshoppers, and are thus distinguished from them." (*New Analytical Bible and Dictionary of the Bible*, page 189.)

The scripture mentions that John's preaching was as a voice crying in the wilderness. As a matter of fact, it was in the wilderness where he did both his teaching and his baptizing.

"These things were done in Bethabara beyond Jordan." (John 1:28.) Matthew says that John baptized in Jordan. (See Matthew 3:13.)

Bethabara is not well known. Some bible scholars say it was "a place east of Jordan, perhaps Bethbara, or rather Bethany."

The *Bible Companion* edited by William Neil for McGraw-Hill says that Bethabara was "another Bethany," not the one where Lazarus and his sisters Mary and Martha lived, but another place "on the left bank of the Jordan, although the exact site is unknown, and here John the Baptist baptized." (Page 272.)

The third chapter of Matthew opens with: "In those days came John the Baptist, preaching in the wilderness of Judea." It also reports that "Jerusalem, and all Judea, and all the region round about Jordan" went out to hear him. Obviously he had a large and mixed audience, ranging from the common people to the scribes and Pharisees, even to the soldiers who came out to maintain order.

Matthew then continues with this important passage:

"Then cometh Jesus from Galilee to Jordan unto John, to be baptized of him.

"But John forbad him, saying, I have need to be baptized of thee, and comest thou to me?

"And Jesus answering said unto him, Suffer it to be so now: for thus it becometh us to fulfil all righteousness. Then he suffered him.

"And Jesus, when he was baptized, went up straightway out of the water: and, lo, the heavens were opened unto him, and he saw the Spirit of God descending like a dove, and lighting upon him:

"And lo a voice from heaven, saying, This is my beloved Son, in whom I am well pleased." (Matthew 3:13-17.)

Thus was Jesus identified by his Heavenly Father. But to whom was the identification made? John's gospel clarifies to some extent:

"The next day John seeth Jesus coming unto him, and saith, Behold the Lamb of God, which taketh away the sin of the world.

"This is he of whom I said, After me cometh a man which is preferred before me: for he was before me.

"And I knew him not: but that he should be made manifest to Israel, therefore am I come baptizing with water.

"And John bare record, saying, I saw the Spirit descending from heaven like a dove, and it abode upon him.

"And I knew him not: but he that sent me to baptize with water, the same said unto me, Upon whom thou shalt see the Spirit descending and remaining on him, the same is he which baptizeth with the Holy Ghost.

"And I saw, and bare record that this is the Son of God.

"Again the next day after John stood, and two of his disciples;

"And looking upon Jesus as he walked, he saith, Behold the Lamb of God!" (John 1:29-36.)

Then the scripture describes the manner in which John's

disciples turned to Christ and began to follow him. The account first refers to only two of them, but it illustrates the point.

Says the sacred word:

"And the two disciples heard him speak, and they followed Jesus.

"Then Jesus turned, and saw them following, and saith unto them, What seek ye? They said unto him, Rabbi, (which is to say, being interpreted, Master,) where dwellest thou?

"He saith unto them, Come and see. They came and saw where he dwelt, and abode with him that day: for it was about the tenth hour.

"One of the two which heard John speak, and followed him, was Andrew, Simon Peter's brother.

"He first findeth his own brother Simon, and saith unto him, We have found the Messias, which is, being interpreted, the Christ." (John 1:37-41.)

In other words, Andrew is here telling his brother Simon that they had found the One of whom John spoke—"the Messias, which is, being interpreted, the Christ."

And then the scripture continues:

"And he brought him to Jesus. And when Jesus beheld him, he said, Thou art Simon the son of Jona: thou shalt be called Cephas, which is by interpretation, A stone." (John 1:42.)

But then is recounted a second instance very much like the first. It shows how John's disciples were turned to Christ, for John had definitely identified the Lord as the Personage of whom he spoke. Says the scripture again:

"The day following Jesus would go forth into Galilee, and findeth Philip, and saith unto him, Follow me.

"Now Philip was of Bethsaida, the city of Andrew and Peter.

"Philip findeth Nathanael, and saith unto him, We have found him, of whom Moses in the law, and the prophets, did write, Jesus of Nazareth, the son of Joseph.

"And Nathanael said unto him, Can there any good thing come out of Nazareth? Philip saith unto him, Come and see.

"Jesus saw Nathanael coming to him, and saith of him, Behold an Israelite indeed, in whom is no guile!

"Nathanael saith unto him, Whence knowest thou me?

Jesus answered and said unto him, Before that Philip called thee, when thou wast under the fig tree, I saw thee.

"Nathanael answered and saith unto him, Rabbi, thou art the Son of God; thou art the King of Israel.

"Jesus answered and said unto him, Because I said unto thee, I saw thee under the fig tree, believest thou? thou shalt see greater things than these.

"And he saith unto him, Verily, verily, I say unto you, Hereafter ye shall see heaven open, and the angels of God ascending and descending upon the Son of man." (John 1:43-51.)

So John prepared the way well. He converted honest men to Christ even before "they had found him"; and when they did find him, they followed him.

Five

"I Must Decrease"

Even after Jesus began his ministry John continually preached of Christ, reiterating his earlier affirmations:

"Ye yourselves bear me witness that I said, I am not the Christ, but that I am sent before him. He that hath the bride is the bridegroom."

He then spoke of himself as the bridegroom's friend and said: "The friend of the bridegroom, which standeth and heareth him, rejoiceth greatly because of the bridegroom's voice: this my joy therefore is fulfilled." (John 3:28-29.)

Thus, in his great humility he took joy even in merely hearing the voice of the Bridegroom whom he knew to be Christ and was happy just to be his friend. What a humble man was John! How well he knew and accepted his position with respect to Jesus!

John knew that the preparation for the Lord had been nearly completed and that his role in this mighty drama would begin to fade as the Savior took the center of the stage. Christ's work, paramount to all other, would now come to fruition. His atonement, soon to be worked out, would be the most important event ever to take place on earth.

Knowing this, John then spoke to his disciples, referring to the Savior, and said:

"He must increase, but I must decrease." (John 3:30.)

It was a remarkable statement of the fitness of things, an example to all mankind. Christ is above all. He is our Lord and our God.

But as John made his remarkable explanation, he also paid a most impressive tribute to his Lord in words not so different from expressions used by the Savior himself. It is one of the most beautiful things in scripture. Said John of Christ:

"He that cometh from above is above all: he that is of the earth is earthly, and speaketh of the earth: he that cometh from heaven is above all.

"And what he hath seen and heard, that he testifieth; and no man receiveth his testimony.

"He that hath received his testimony hath set to his seal that God is true.

"For he whom God hath sent speaketh the words of God: for God giveth not the Spirit by measure unto him.

"The Father loveth the Son, and hath given all things into his hand.

"He that believeth on the Son hath everlasting life: and he that believeth not the Son shall not see life; but the wrath of God abideth on him." (John 3:31-36.)

John continued his work, baptizing in Aenon near to Salim, "because there was much water there." (John 3:23.) But:

"Jesus made and baptized more disciples than John,

"(Though Jesus himself baptized not, but his disciples)." (John 4:1-2.)

So John began to "decrease." But he did not decline in courage or vigor; for when Herod the king unlawfully took his brother's wife, John rebuked him for it and as a result was cast into prison.

Herod the tetrarch was an evil man. Having heard of the fame of Christ who was beginning his ministry, the king at first supposed that Jesus was the Baptist come back to life, for he had put John to death for his rebuke.

Matthew tells the story in these words:

"At that time Herod the tetrarch heard of the fame of Jesus,

"And said unto his servants, This is John the Baptist; he is risen from the dead; and therefore mighty works do shew forth themselves in him.

"For Herod had laid hold on John, and bound him, and put him in prison for Herodias' sake, his brother Philip's wife.

"For John said unto him, It is not lawful for thee to have her.

"And when he would have put him to death, he feared the multitude, because they counted him as a prophet.

"But when Herod's birthday was kept, the daughter of Herodias danced before them, and pleased Herod.

"Whereupon he promised with an oath to give her whatsoever she would ask.

"And she, being before instructed of her mother, said, Give me here John Baptist's head in a charger.

"And the king was sorry: nevertheless for the oath's sake, and them which sat with him at meat, he commanded it to be given her.

"And he sent, and beheaded John in the prison.

"And his head was brought in a charger, and given to the damsel: and she brought it to her mother.

"And his disciples came, and took up the body, and buried it, and went and told Jesus." (Matthew 14:1-12.)

So John completed his work, and what a mighty mission it was! He had opened the door to the Christian era. He had prepared the way for the Christ, the Author of that Christian era, and had given his life for the cause of his divine cousin, the Creator of the world. As the Lord's forerunner in mortality, John was superb.

PART TWO

THE PREPARATION FOR THE SECOND COMING

Six

The Last Dispensation

The Savior's mortal advent and his personal introduction of Christianity ended eventually in an apostasy from his great truth. Mankind wrote creeds of their own, different from his gospel, and formed their own churches with new rituals and self-appointed clergy. As Isaiah said so clearly:

"The earth also is defiled under the inhabitants thereof; because they have transgressed the laws, changed the ordinance, broken the everlasting covenant." (Isaiah 24:5.)

This apostasy had been predicted by various of the early Brethren, particularly by Paul and Peter. Jesus himself said that there would be false Christs and false prophets who would "shew great signs and wonders; insomuch that, if it were possible, they shall deceive the very elect." (Matthew 24:24.)

Paul said: "For I know this, that after my departing shall grievous wolves enter in among you, not sparing the flock.

"Also of your own selves shall men arise, speaking perverse things, to draw away disciples after them." (Acts 20:29-30.)

And he told Timothy:

"Now the Spirit speaketh expressly, that in the latter times some shall depart from the faith, giving heed to seducing spirits, and doctrines of devils;

"Speaking lies in hypocrisy; having their conscience seared with a hot iron;

"Forbidding to marry, and commanding to abstain from meats, which God hath created to be received with thanksgiving of them which believe and know the truth.

"For every creature of God is good, and nothing to be refused, if it be received with thanksgiving." (1 Timothy 4:1-4.)

Peter, discoursing on the same subject, wrote:

"But there were false prophets also among the people, even as there shall be false teachers among you, who privily shall bring in damnable heresies, even denying the Lord that bought them, and bring upon themselves swift destruction.

"And many shall follow their pernicious ways; by reason of whom the way of truth shall be evil spoken of.

"And through covetousness shall they with feigned words make merchandise of you: whose judgment now of a long time lingereth not, and their damnation slumbereth not." (2 Peter 2:1-3.)

And Jude said:

"But, beloved, remember ye the words which were spoken before of the apostles of our Lord Jesus Christ;

"How that they told you there should be mockers in the last time, who should walk after their own ungodly lusts.

"These be they who separate themselves, sensual, having not the Spirit." (Jude 17-19.)

Paul saw apostasy begin among his own converts and therefore wrote to the Galatians:

"I marvel that ye are so soon removed from him that called you into the grace of Christ unto another gospel:

"Which is not another; but there be some that trouble you, and would pervert the gospel of Christ.

"But though we, or an angel from heaven, preach any other gospel unto you than that which we have preached unto you, let him be accursed." (Galatians 1:6-8.)

And he wrote to the Thessalonians:

"For the mystery of iniquity doth already work: only he who now letteth will let, until he be taken out of the way.

"And then shall that Wicked be revealed, whom the Lord shall consume with the spirit of his mouth, and shall destroy with the brightness of his coming:

"Even him, whose coming is after the working of Satan with all power and signs and lying wonders,

"And with all deceivableness of unrighteousness in them that perish; because they received not the love of the truth, that they might be saved.

"And for this cause God shall send them strong delusion, that they should believe a lie." (2 Thessalonians 2:7-11.)

And when he wrote to Titus he said:

"For there are many unruly and vain talkers and deceivers, specially they of the circumcision:

"Whose mouths must be stopped, who subvert whole houses, teaching things which they ought not, for filthy lucre's sake.

"Unto the pure all things are pure: but unto them that are defiled and unbelieving is nothing pure; but even their mind and conscience is defiled.

"They profess that they know God; but in works they deny him, being abominable, and disobedient, and unto every good work reprobate." (Titus 1:10-11, 15-16.)

The Apostle John wrote similarly:

"Little children, it is the last time: and as ye have heard that antichrist shall come, even now are there many antichrists; whereby we know that it is the last time.

"They went out from us, but they were not of us; for if they had been of us, they would no doubt have continued with us: but they went out, that they might be made manifest that they were not all of us." (1 John 2:18-19.)

And in his second letter to Timothy, Paul wrote:

"This know also, that in the last days perilous times shall come.

"For men shall be lovers of their own selves, covetous, boasters, proud, blasphemers, disobedient to parents, unthankful, unholy.

"Without natural affection, trucebreakers, false accusers, incontinent, fierce, despisers of those that are good,

"Traitors, heady, highminded, lovers of pleasures more than lovers of God;

"Having a form of godliness, but denying the power thereof: from such turn away.

"For of this sort are they which creep into houses, and lead captive silly women laden with sins, led away with divers lusts,

"Ever learning, and never able to come to the knowledge of the truth." (2 Timothy 3:1-7.)

In those days so much was said about the second coming of Christ that many supposed it would occur in the day in which they themselves lived. But this was not so, the Brethren explained to the Saints. It must come later.

When Paul discussed this with the Thessalonians, he wrote:

"Now we beseech you, brethren, by the coming of our Lord Jesus Christ, and by our gathering together unto him,

"That ye be not soon shaken in mind, or be troubled, neither by spirit, nor by word, nor by letter as from us, as that the day of Christ is at hand.

"Let no man deceive you by any means: for that day shall not come, except there come a falling away first, and that man of sin be revealed, the son of perdition;

"Who opposeth and exalteth himself above all that is called God, or that is worshipped; so that he as God sitteth in the temple of God, shewing himself that he is God." (2 Thessalonians 2:1-4.)

When this passage was translated by the Roman Catholic scholars as they produced their New American Bible (1972), they gave this rendering:

"We beg you, brothers, not to be so easily agitated or terrified . . . into believing that the day of the Lord is here. Let no one seduce you . . . since the mass apostasy has not yet occurred."

With this passage the translators provided the following footnote in this Bible:

"They should not allow themselves to be duped into this way of thinking, for a religious apostasy is destined to precede the Lord's second coming."

In 1947, following the Second World War, the Catholic Church produced a new version of the Bible in Great Britain. In this reference in 2 Thessalonians the Bible states that the Second Coming would not occur until after a great religious revolt had taken place. Their scholars also provided this footnote:

"A revolt, or rather the revolt. The Greek places the article before the word *apostasia*. This seems to refer to a great apostasy from the Christian faith preceding Christ's return."

Another Catholic Bible, that translated by Knox, renders this passage in 2 Thessalonians as:

"Do not let anyone lead you astray. The apostasy must come first."

From the Coneybeare version in the Epistles of St. Paul we read: "Before that day the falling away must first have come."

From the Weymouth version (The New Testament in Modern Speech): "For it cannot come unless the apostasy comes first."

From the Williams version of the New Testament: "For that cannot take place until the great revolt occurs."

From the Twentieth Century New Testament: "For it will not come until after the Great Apostasy."

From Taylor's *Living Letters*: "For that day will not come until two things happen: first there will be a time of great rebellion against God."

The Literal Translation of the Greek New Testament by Dr. George Ricker Barry of the University of Chicago and Colgate University, departments of Semitic languages, renders the passage like this, as a literal word-for-word translation of the original text:

"Now we beseech you brethren by the coming of our Lord Jesus Christ and our gathering together unto him, for not quickly to be shaken you in mind nor to be troubled, neither by spirit, nor by word, nor by epistle, as if by us, as that is present the day of the Christ. Not anyone you should deceive in any way, because it will not be unless shall have come the apostasy first."

From the New English Bible, we have: "Let no one deceive you in any way whatever. That day cannot come before the final rebellion against God."

And from Schonfield's Authentic New Testament we have: "It will not begin before the Defection has first taken place."

So there can be no doubt, from the scripture, that the second coming of Christ will not occur until after a universal apostasy from the true Christian faith has taken place.

The existence of hundreds of different Christian churches is itself ample evidence of such a falling away. Christ, who said that there is but one strait gate and narrow way, who organized but one Church and prayed that his disciples might be one even as the Father and the Son are one, could never accept the maze of conflicting creeds and practices now present in so-called Christian churches. (See John 17; Matthew 7:13-14.)

Paul taught that "there is but one body, and one Spirit, even as ye are called in one hope of your calling; One Lord, one faith [or true gospel], one baptism, One God and Father of all." (Ephesians 4:4-6.) He could not endorse the apostasy which he saw develop in his own time.

Paul told the Corinthians, who were splitting up into factions and denominations:

"Now I beseech you, brethren, by the name of our Lord Jesus Christ, that ye all speak the same thing, and that there be no divisions among you; but that ye be perfectly joined together in the same mind and in the same judgment.

"For it hath been declared unto me of you, my brethren, by them which are of the house of Chloe, that there are contentions among you.

"Now this I say, that every one of you saith, I am of Paul; and I of Apollos; and I of Cephas; and I of Christ.

"Is Christ divided? was Paul crucified for you? or were ye baptized in the name of Paul?" (1 Corinthians 1:10-13.)

So the great apostasy had begun even in the days of the apostles, and they fought heroically against it. Nearly all of the epistles in the New Testament were written to combat it. The book of Revelation confirmed it. When each of the seven churches or branches of the Church was addressed, the condition was made known even further. As the Saints at Ephesus, once a stronghold of the faith, were addressed, what was said?

"Thou hast left thy first love. Remember therefore from whence thou art fallen."

The Saints at Smyrna were warned against "the blasphemy of them which say they are Jews and are not, but are the synagogue of Satan."

The Saints at Pergamos were told to guard against the doctrines of Balaam and were reminded that "so hast thou also them that hold to the doctrine of the Nicolaitans, which thing I hate. Repent; or else I will come unto thee quickly, and will fight against them with the sword of my mouth."

To those at Thyatira it was said, "I have a few things against thee, because thou sufferest that woman Jezebel, which calleth herself a prophetess, to teach and to seduce my servants to commit fornication."

To those at Sardis came the word: "I have not found thy works perfect before God," and those at Philadelphia received a similar rebuke. To the Laodiceans there came: "I know thy work, that thou art neither cold nor hot: I would thou wert cold or hot. So then because thou art lukewarm, and neither cold nor hot, I will spue thee out of my mouth." (Revelation 2, 3.)

But what was the Lord to do? Would he allow his work to be forever lost in wickedness? Would he allow Satan "that old serpent, even the devil, who rebelled against God, and sought to take the kingdom of our God and his Christ" (D&C 76:28) to gain a permanent victory?

John the Revelator declared that although the devil will make war against Christ, "the Lamb shall overcome," for, he added, "he is Lord of lords and King of kings." (Revelation 17:14.)

Then what would the Lord do?

He would restore his gospel and raise up new prophets, and the gospel would be taken to all the world by them as a witness to all nations, and then—and then only—shall the end come. (See Matthew 24.)

How would the gospel be restored?

The matter comes back again to the premise of the Prophet Amos. The Lord will work through prophets. Otherwise, he will do *nothing*.

He loves modern peoples as much as he did the ancients and determines to offer salvation to them also, since he is no respector of persons.

The Apostle Peter discoursed about the second coming of Christ and promised that before that glorious event there would be a restoration of the gospel.

This restoration was to be universal in two ways: It would include "all that God hath spoken by the mouth of all his holy prophets since the world began," and it would "be preached in all the world for a witness unto all nations, and then the end [would] come."

The latter promise was made by the Lord himself (see Matthew 24:14), and the former by Peter in his notable address at the gate Beautiful of the temple. (See Acts 3:21.)

Peter and John had healed a cripple there. In his rejoicing, the beggar leaped and caused such a commotion that the people in the temple gathered around to see what it was all about. In a powerful address, Peter told them the miracle was brought about by the power of that Christ "whom ye delivered up, and denied him in the presence of Pilate, when he was determined to let him go. And killed the Prince of life, whom God hath raised from the dead, whereof we are witnesses."

Sensing an important fact, Peter continued, "And now, brethren, I wot that through ignorance ye did it, as did also your rulers." And hence, he called them to repentance and promised them that Christ would come again.

He explained that the Lord would not come in his second advent "until the times of restitution of all things, which God hath spoken by the mouth of all his holy prophets since the world began."

It was a most significant statement. To bring back all things that God had spoken through his prophets since the beginning of the world meant, indeed, a universal restitution.

What is already present cannot be restored. The gospel could not come back to earth if it were already here. To restore it would require that it had been lost, and so it was. But how was it lost? It was through the manufacture of man-made religions and creeds and the creation of hundreds of churches built upon the caprice of human desires and practices.

Other Bible versions sustain the King James in this passage on the restoration. The Revised Version of 1952 says: "Whom heaven must receive until the time for establishing all that God spoke by the mouth of his holy prophets from of old."

The Knox Catholic Bible of 1955 says: "Then he will send Jesus Christ who has now been made known unto you, but must have his dwelling place in heaven until the time when all is restored anew."

The American Standard version speaks of it as "the restoration of all things." The Rotherham version: "The due establishment of all things." The Twentieth Century: "The universal restoration"; and the Weymouth version: "The re-constitution of all things."

This last-mentioned reference, from the Weymouth Bible, is an interesting rendering — "the re-constitution of all things." It gives the thought of re-doing the work, of re-building the kingdom, of re-constituting or re-structuring that which was once here and then lost. And that is the precise situation.

When the Knox version says that it will be a time "when all is restored anew," again the actual facts are portrayed. It will be made like it was when it was newly given. Now it will be restored anew—made new again, and useful, and powerful, and able to save.

And how was it to come? By means of an angel flying through the heavens, bringing the gospel back to earth, in the hour of God's judgment, to be preached to all nations. (See Revelation 14:6-7.)

Other versions of the Bible also make this abundantly clear. Says the New English Bible:

"Then I saw an angel flying in mid-heaven with an eternal gospel to proclaim to those on earth, to every nation and tribe, language and people. He cried in a loud voice, Fear God, and pay him homage, for the hour of his judgment is come."

The Standard Revised Version says: "Then I saw another angel flying in mid-heaven with an eternal gospel to proclaim to those who dwell on earth, to every nation, and tribe and tongue and people."

The Philips version says: "Then I saw another angel flying in mid-heaven holding the everlasting gospel to proclaim to the inhabitants of the earth, to every nation and tribe and language and people."

Moffatt says: "Then I saw another angel flying in mid-heaven with an eternal gospel for the inhabitants of the earth, for every nation and tribe and tongue and people."

The New World (Jehovah's Witnesses) Bible says: "And I saw another angel flying in mid-heaven and he had everlasting good news to declare as glad tidings to those who dwell on the earth, and to every nation and tribe and tongue and people."

Knox says: "I saw too, another angel flying in mid-heaven carrying with him a final gospel to preach to all those who dwell on the earth, to every race, and tribe, and language and people."

The Arendzen Catholic Bible says: "And I saw another angel flying through the midst of heaven having the eternal gospel to preach unto them that sit upon the earth and over every nation and tribe and tongue and people."

Billy Graham's Bible reads on this point: "And I saw another angel flying through the heavens, carrying the everlasting Good News to preach to those on earth—to every nation, tribe, language and people."

Obviously the Bible means what it says. There was destined to be a restoration of all that God had ever spoken through his prophets. It would come in latter days "in the hour of God's judgment." It would go to all the world as a witness to all nations before the end comes, and it *would be brought to earth by an angel.*

This was to be the new dispensation—the final dispensation—of the gospel as spoken of by the prophets. Of this Paul said to the Ephesians:

"He hath abounded toward us in all wisdom and prudence;

"Having made known unto us the mystery of his will, according to his good pleasure which he hath purposed in himself:

"That in the dispensation of the fulness of times he might gather together in one all things in Christ, both which are in heaven and which are on earth; even in him." (Ephesians 1:8-10.)

His reference to the dispensation of the "fulness of times," of course, parallels Peter's prediction that "all things which God hath spoken by the mouth of *all his holy prophets since the world began*" should be restored.

All those things were to be brought together, thus constituting the "fulness of times"—the inclusion of all previous times, everything to be re-assembled. That was to be the dispensation of the gospel thus spoken of.

But to whom would the angel come? Who would bring forth this "fulness of all times," the final dispensation of the gospel before the end comes?

Again we remember Amos. These events would have to include the services of a prophet, for otherwise the Lord God will do nothing. With no prophets on earth because of apostasy, God would now have to raise up a new one in order to fulfill His purposes.

Seven

A New Prophet Comes

God had prepared well for his last dispensation of the gospel. A large part of that preparation was the setting up of the United States as a free and independent country where the gospel could be restored. Through a constitution which was written by men divinely raised up for this very purpose, he provided freedom of religion, assembly, press, and speech.

The colonists who had come here were religious people for the most part. Many came to America to escape the monarchical conditions abroad and to make their homes in this land where they could worship God according to the dictates of their own consciences.

With such freedom established here, the Lord was ready to introduce the gospel to mankind once again. Since he works only through prophets and since no prophets were on earth at this time, he found it necessary to raise up a new one—which he did.

From the preexistent world, he sent to earth—to be born on December 23, 1805, in Sharon, Windsor County, Vermont—one of his choice spirits to assume the great burden of restoration.

This choice spirit was Joseph Smith, Jr., son of Joseph Smith, Sr., and Lucy Mack Smith. He was the third son and fourth child in a family of ten children. His parents were of sturdy New England stock—honest, God-fearing, and industrious, but poor in this world's goods.

His forebears emigrated from England in 1638. Some of his ancestors took part in the American War of Independence under the command of General George Washington.

The family members were farmers and tradesmen, living at first in Vermont and later in western New York near the city of Palmyra. It was there that the Lord made himself known to the boy Joseph.

In the spring of 1820 when Joseph was but fourteen years old, he was moved upon to seek the Lord in prayer. Much religious confusion existed in the community, and his own family was divided as to religious affiliation.

Since the Lord's appointed time had come for the restoration of the gospel, Joseph, the chosen instrument, was moved by the Holy Spirit to open the family Bible and read from James:

"If any of you lack wisdom, let him ask of God, that giveth to all men liberally, and upbraideth not; and it shall be given him." (1:5.)

Still influenced by the Holy Spirit, Joseph resolved to pray for that wisdom.

Let no one suppose that this was an ordinary desire of an ordinary person to learn which church was right. The last dispensation was about to open. The Lord was in charge. It was he who influenced the young man to read that Bible passage. It was He who brought him into a nearby grove in humble prayer.

And it was He—at this crucial moment in modern history —who appeared to that boy whom He had sent from the pre-existence for this very purpose and who now knelt before Him seeking wisdom.

The Almighty God, Father of us all, and his Most Beloved Son, the Lord Jesus Christ, our Savior, came down from their courts on high and stood before that young man in a holy visitation.

He could see them and hear them, for they spoke to him.

Never before was there a recorded visitation of both Father and Son appearing at the same time to the same mortal person. But now they came—together—and the Father said: "Joseph, this is my Beloved Son, hear Him."

Joseph had desired to know which church in the community he should join. The Father deferred to the Son who gave the answer: "None of them."

And why? Because they were man-made; they taught for doctrines the commandments of men; their creeds were an abomination in his sight. The Almighty neither recognized nor acknowledged any of the denominations as his own. His true Church was lost to mortal men, who did not so much as know what God was like. So how could they worship him intelligently? The apostasy had been complete.

For centuries mankind had believed the uninspired creeds which described the Deity as a shapeless, indefinable non-Person who was everywhere at once and was incomprehensible to mortals.

Since the gospel was now to be restored for the last time, it would have to be founded upon a correct knowledge of the nature of God. So this vital knowledge was restored in this first vision of Joseph Smith. The boy gazed upon the faces and figures of these two divine Beings and could see that in fact they were Persons, that they were separate Individuals as all people are separate from one another, and that in fact man was made in their likeness. They appeared as men appear. Except that they were glorified, they were in the image and likeness of mortals. Joseph now knew that man was truly made in the image and likeness of God, just as the Bible taught.

What a marvelous experience! What an important revelation this was! What light had now come into the world! A mortal man again had seen the Father and the Son and talked with them face to face. At last, after all the dark centuries, someone on earth knew the nature of God, that he was not some formless essence floating throughout the universe, but that he was an intelligent, glorified, celestialized Person.

This great revelation was prerequisite to the restoration of the gospel. Of what value would further teaching be if the Object of our worship were to remain a mystery?

We must know God to worship him intelligently. This vision revealing his nature opened the door for the last dispensation of the gospel. Through the vision Joseph also was called to be a modern prophet.

The Lord had now prepared for the coming of the angel who was assigned to restore the gospel. There would be a prophet on earth to receive the angel and all would be in harmony with the words of Amos:

"Surely the Lord God will do nothing, but he revealeth his secret unto his servants the prophets." (Amos 3:7.)

Eight

The Angel Comes

John the Revelator saw in vision the opening of this final dispensation of the gospel. Said he:

"And I saw another angel fly in the midst of heaven, having the everlasting gospel to preach unto them that dwell on the earth, and to every nation, and kindred, and tongue, and people,

"Saying with a loud voice, Fear God, and give glory to him; for the hour of his judgment is come: and worship him that made heaven, and earth, and the sea, and the fountains of water." (Revelation 14:6-7.)

Amid heavenly light this angel came to the Joseph Smith home near Palmyra, New York, on the night of September 21, 1823, and there informed the young man of the great events soon to transpire.

But he was not the only angel to come. Was not everything to be restored whatsoever God had spoken by all his holy prophets from the beginning of the world? (See Acts 3:21.)

What others came, and why? They were:

John the Baptist, conferring upon Joseph Smith and Oliver Cowdery the Aaronic Priesthood, with the power to baptize.

Peter, James, and John, giving them the Melchizedek Priesthood and the holy apostleship.

Moses, giving them power to gather Israel in these last days.

Elijah, conferring on them the powers which turn the hearts of fathers and children toward each other, to form a patriarchal order for all eternity.

Elias, who brought the keys related to the gospel dispensation of Abraham. (See D&C 110.)

Michael, or Adam, detecting the devil when he appeared as an angel of light.

Gabriel, who was Noah of the flood; Raphael, "and . . . divers angels, from Michael or Adam down to the present time, all declaring their dispensations, their rights, their keys, their honors, their majesty and glory, and the power of their priesthood, giving line upon line, precept upon precept, here a little, and there a little, giving us consolation by holding forth that which is to come, confirming our hope!" (D&C 128:21.)

The other dispensations now were consolidated into one, and all "which God hath spoken by the mouth of all his holy prophets since the world began" was thus restored. (Acts 3:21.)

The prophecies were fulfilled. Preparation was made to carry the gospel into all the world before the second coming of Christ. (See Matthew 24.) The preparer of the way was the new, modern prophet, raised up in his childhood, unspoiled by the teachings of men, Joseph Smith, Jr.

He was the one chosen in these last days to be the forerunner of the Savior, even as John the Baptist was chosen to prepare the way for the first coming of the Lord.

What great missions John and Joseph had! What suffering they both endured! How faithful and devoted they were! And how completely they fulfilled their charge, both closing their labors in martyrdom!

John, who introduced Christ to the world, was named by the Savior as one of our greatest prophets.

Joseph was declared to have done more for the salvation of mankind than any other person who ever lived on earth with the sole exception of Jesus Christ, the Savior himself.

Had not Malachi foreseen his work? He wrote:

"Behold, I will send my messenger, and he shall prepare the way before me: and the Lord, whom ye seek, shall suddenly come to his temple, even the messenger of the covenant, whom ye delight in: behold, he shall come, saith the Lord of hosts." (Malachi 3:1.)

Joseph was the Lord's forerunner—his messenger—chosen as the instrument of heaven through whom the gospel would be restored in "the hour of God's judgment."

What was restored in these last days? How will we recognize it? How may we know for sure which church is right? What are the signs of the true church whereby it may be identified with certainty?

Nine

The Nature of God

From early Christian times the true nature of God was lost, and men groped in the darkness as they formulated varied ideas concerning what he was like.

Some patterned their definitions after the Roman and Greek deities, since both Roman and Greek influence was strong from the final dispersion of the Jews in A.D. 70 and for several centuries thereafter.

Men sometimes thought of the Christian God as only the Father, at another time as only the Son, and at other times as only the Holy Ghost. Yet they were all three considered as one God in three, and it was admittedly incomprehensible. The idea also became extant that God was a formless essence distributed throughout all creation, with no body, no shape, no parts, no passions.

Even the Eastern notion of Deity was introduced by some saying that he was universal, formless intelligence; and that when we die, our immortality consists of being absorbed into the universal intelligence, thus losing our own personalities, our own individuality.

The creeds of the various denominations centered largely on such definitions, causing complete confusion as to the nature of Deity in the minds of Christians everywhere.

How could they worship him in spirit and in truth when they did not have the truth?

A restoration of the true knowledge of God was all-important.

What is God like?

As Joseph Smith gazed upon the Father and the Son in his first vision, he discovered their true nature. He said:

"I saw two Personages, whose brightness and glory defy all description, standing above me in the air. One of them spake unto me, calling me by name and said, pointing to the other— *This is My Beloved Son. Hear Him!*

"My object in going to inquire of the Lord was to know which of all the sects was right, that I might know which to join. No sooner, therefore, did I get possession of myself, so as to be able to speak, than I asked the Personages who stood above me in the light, which of all the sects was right—and which I should join.

"I was answered that I must join none of them, for they were all wrong; and the Personage who addressed me said that all their creeds were an abomination in his sight; that those professors were all corrupt; that: 'they draw near to me with their lips, but their hearts are far from me, they teach for doctrines the commandments of men, having a form of godliness, but they deny the power thereof.'

"He again forbade me to join with any of them; and many other things did he say unto me, which I cannot write at this time."

Later on he was persecuted for saying that he had seen the Father and the Son. Of this he wrote:

"It caused me serious reflection then, and often has since, how very strange it was that an obscure boy, of a little over fourteen years of age, and one, too, who was doomed to the necessity of obtaining a scanty maintenance by his daily labor, should be thought a character of sufficient importance to attract the attention of the great ones of the most popular sects of the day, and in a manner to create in them a spirit of the most bitter persecution and reviling. But strange or not, so it was, and it was often the cause of great sorrow to myself.

"However, it was nevertheless a fact that I had beheld a vision. I have thought since, that I felt much like Paul, when he made his defense before King Agrippa, and related the account of the vision he had when he saw a light, and heard a voice; but still there were but few who believed him; some said he was dishonest, others said he was mad; and he was ridiculed and reviled. But all this did not destroy the reality of his vision. He had seen a vision, he knew he had, and all the persecution under heaven could not make it otherwise; and though they should persecute him unto death, yet he knew, and would know to his latest breath, that he had both seen a light and heard a voice speaking unto him, and all the world could not make him think or believe otherwise.

"So it was with me. I had actually seen a light, and in the midst of that light I saw two Personages, and they did in reality speak to me; and though I was hated and persecuted for saying that I had seen a vision, yet it was true; and while they were persecuting me, reviling me, and speaking all manner of evil against me falsely for so saying, I was led to say in my heart: Why persecute me for telling the truth? I have actually seen a vision; and who am I that I can withstand God, or why does the world think to make me deny what I have actually seen? For I had seen a vision; I knew it, and I knew that God knew it, and I could not deny it, neither dared I do it; at least I knew that by so doing I would offend God, and come under condemnation.

"I had now got my mind satisfied so far as the sectarian world was concerned—that it was not my duty to join with any of them, but to continue as I was until further directed. I had found the testimony of James to be true—that a man who lacked wisdom might ask of God, and obtain, and not be upbraided." (Joseph Smith 2:17-20, 23-26.)

Subsequently he saw a vision of the Savior which is recorded by himself and Oliver Cowdery in this language:

"The veil was taken from our minds, and the eyes of our understanding were opened.

"We saw the Lord standing upon the breastwork of the pulpit, before us; and under his feet was a paved work of pure gold, in color like amber.

"His eyes were as a flame of fire; the hair of his head was white like the pure snow; his countenance shone above the brightness of the sun; and his voice was as the sound of the rushing of great waters, even the voice of Jehovah, saying:

"I am the first and the last; I am he who liveth, I am he who was slain; I am your advocate with the Father.

"Behold, your sins are forgiven you; you are clean before me; therefore, lift up your heads and rejoice.

"Let the hearts of your brethren rejoice, and let the hearts of all my people rejoice, who have, with their might, built this house to my name.

"For behold, I have accepted this house, and my name shall be here; and I will manifest myself to my people in mercy in this house.

"Yea, I will appear unto my servants, and speak unto them with mine own voice, if my people will keep my commandments, and do not pollute this holy house." (D&C 110:1-8.)

On still another occasion, this time while he was with Sidney Rigdon, Joseph Smith again beheld the Father and the Son and wrote of them as follows:

"Speaking of the resurrection of the dead, concerning those who shall hear the voice of the Son of Man, and shall come forth—

"They who have done good in the resurrection of the just, and they who have done evil in the resurrection of the unjust—

"Now this caused us to marvel, for it was given unto us of the Spirit.

"And while we meditated upon these things, the Lord touched the eyes of our understandings and they were opened, and the glory of the Lord shone round about.

"And we beheld the glory of the Son, on the right hand of the Father, and received of his fulness;

"And saw the holy angels, and them who are sanctified before his throne, worshiping God, and the Lamb, who worship him forever and ever.

"And now, after the many testimonies which have been given of him, this is the testimony, last of all, which we give of him: That he lives!

"For we saw him, even on the right hand of God; and we heard the voice bearing record that he is the Only Begotten of the Father—

"That by him, and through him, and of him, the worlds are and were created, and the inhabitants thereof are begotten sons and daughters unto God." (D&C 76:16-24.)

In the Kirtland Temple the Prophet Joseph was again given a vision of the Father and the Son, of which he wrote:

"I beheld the celestial kingdom of God, and the glory thereof, whether in the body or out I cannot tell.

"I saw the transcendent beauty of the gate through which the heirs of that kingdom will enter, which was like unto circling flames of fire;

"Also the blazing throne of God, whereon was seated the Father and the Son.

"I saw the beautiful streets of that kingdom, which had the appearance of being paved with gold.

"I saw Fathers Adam and Abraham; and my father and my mother; my brother Alvin, that has long since slept;

"And marveled how it was that he had obtained an inheritance in the kingdom, seeing that he had departed this life before the Lord had set his hand to gather Israel the second time, and had not been baptized for the remission of sins.

"Thus came the voice of the Lord to me, saying: All who have died without a knowledge of this gospel, who would have received it if they had been permitted to tarry, shall be heirs of the celestial kingdom of God;

"Also all that shall die henceforth without a knowledge of it, who would have received it with all their hearts, shall be heirs of that kingdom;

"For I, the Lord, will judge all men according to their works, according to the desire of their hearts.

"And I also beheld that all children who die before they arrive at the years of accountability are saved in the celestial kingdom of heaven." (D&C 137, new edition.)

President Joseph Fielding Smith in *Essentials in Church History* (Deseret Book Company), adds this to his account of the dedication of the Kirtland Temple:

"As soon as the Temple was dedicated, ordinance work for the elders was commenced. The ordinance of washing of feet—which the Prophet said was never intended but for the official members of the Church—was attended to in behalf of the leading quorums, and other ordinances were performed. *The Savior appeared to several of the brethren and angels ministered to others in these meetings.* It was indeed a time of Pentecost to the Saints." (Page 159. Italics added.)

Was not the true nature of God made abundantly evident to the Prophet Joseph Smith as well as to some of his brethren? Who could doubt it?

The events in Kirtland were reminiscent of the time when Moses took the seventy elders of ancient Israel into the mount where "they saw the God of Israel: and there was under his feet as it were a paved work of a sapphire stone, and as it were the body of heaven in his clearness.

"And upon the nobles of the children of Israel he laid not his hand: also they saw God, and did eat and drink." (Exodus 24:10-11.)

Modern scripture also establishes further that God conversed freely with Moses, who saw him face to face and talked with him. Moses spent forty days in the presence of the Lord.

The Lord revealed to Joseph Smith Moses' words about God and creation. Among those writings we have:

"The words of God, which he spake unto Moses at a time when Moses was caught up into an exceedingly high mountain,

"And he saw God face to face, and he talked with him, and the glory of God was upon Moses; therefore Moses could endure his presence.

"And God spake unto Moses, saying: Behold, I am the Lord God Almighty, and Endless is my name; for I am without beginning of days or end of years; and is not this endless?

"And, behold, thou art my son; wherefore look, and I will show thee the workmanship of mine hands; but not all, for my works are without end, and also my words, for they never cease.

"Wherefore, no man can behold all my works, except he behold all my glory, and no man can behold all my glory, and afterwards remain in the flesh on the earth.

"And I have a work for thee, Moses, my son; and thou art in the similitude of mine Only Begotten; and mine Only Begotten is and shall be the Savior, for he is full of grace and truth; but there is no God beside me, and all things are present with me, for I know them all.

"And now, behold, this one thing I show unto thee, Moses, my son; for thou art in the world, and now I show it unto thee.

"And it came to pass that Moses looked, and beheld the world upon which he was created; and Moses beheld the world and the ends thereof, and all the children of men which are, and which were created; of the same he greatly marveled and wondered.

"And the presence of God withdrew from Moses, that his glory was not upon Moses; and Moses was left unto himself. And as he was left unto himself, he fell unto the earth.

"And it came to pass that it was for the space of many hours before Moses did again receive his natural strength like unto man; and he said unto himself: Now, for this cause I know that man is nothing, which thing I never had supposed.

"But now mine own eyes have beheld God; but not my natural, but my spiritual eyes, for my natural eyes could not have beheld; for I should have withered and died in his presence; but his glory was upon me; and I beheld his face, for I was transfigured before him." (Moses 1:1-11.)

Following this, Moses told more of this experience. It was revealed to Joseph Smith by the Lord as part of the restoration of all things:

"And calling upon the name of God, he beheld his glory again, for it was upon him; and he heard a voice, saying: Blessed art thou, Moses, for I, the Almighty, have chosen thee, and thou shalt be made stronger than many waters; for they shall obey thy command as if thou wert God.

"And lo, I am with thee, even unto the end of thy days; for thou shalt deliver my people from bondage, even Israel my chosen.

"And it came to pass, as the voice was still speaking, Moses cast his eyes and beheld the earth, yea, even all of it; and there was not a particle of it which he did not behold, discerning it by the Spirit of God.

"And he beheld also the inhabitants thereof, and there was not a soul which he beheld not; and he discerned them by the Spirit of God; and their numbers were great, even numberless as the sand upon the sea shore.

"And he beheld many lands; and each land was called earth, and there were inhabitants on the face thereof.

"And it came to pass that Moses called upon God, saying: Tell me, I pray thee, why these things are so, and by what thou madest them?

"And behold, the glory of the Lord was upon Moses, so that Moses stood in the presence of God, and talked with him face to face. And the Lord God said unto Moses: For mine own purpose have I made these things. Here is wisdom and it remaineth in me.

"And by the word of my power, have I created them, which is mine Only Begotten Son, who is full of grace and truth.

"And worlds without number have I created; and I also created them for mine own purpose; and by the Son I created them, which is mine Only Begotten." (Moses 1:25-33.)

As part of the restoration of the gospel, the Lord provided us with the Book of Mormon. It, too, contains much information concerning the personality and nature of both Christ, the Son, and of God, the Father.

Note the following from 3 Nephi, describing the coming of the Savior to the Nephites:

"And now it came to pass that there were a great multitude gathered together, of the people of Nephi, round about the temple which was in the land Bountiful; and they were marveling and wondering one with another, and were showing one to another the great and marvelous change which had taken place.

"And they were also conversing about this Jesus Christ, of whom the sign had been given concerning his death.

"And it came to pass that while they were thus conversing one with another, they heard a voice as if it came out of heaven;

and they cast their eyes round about, for they understood not the voice which they heard; and it was not a harsh voice, neither was it a loud voice; nevertheless, and notwithstanding it being a small voice it did pierce them that did hear to the center, insomuch that there was no part of their frame that it did not cause to quake; yea, it did pierce them to the very soul, and did cause their hearts to burn.

"And it came to pass that again they heard the voice, and they understood it not.

"And again the third time they did hear the voice, and did open their ears to hear it; and their eyes were towards the sound thereof; and they did look steadfastly towards heaven, from whence the sound came.

"And behold, the third time they did understand the voice which they heard; and it said unto them:

"Behold my Beloved Son, in whom I am well pleased, in whom I have glorified my name—hear ye him.

"And it came to pass, as they understood they cast their eyes up again towards heaven; and behold, they saw a Man descending out of heaven; and he was clothed in a white robe; and he came down and stood in the midst of them; and the eyes of the whole multitude were turned upon him, and they durst not open their mouths, even one to another, and wist not what it meant, for they thought it was an angel that had appeared unto them.

"And it came to pass that he stretched forth his hand and spake unto the people, saying:

"Behold, I am Jesus Christ, whom the prophets testified shall come into the world.

"And behold, I am the light and the life of the world; and I have drunk out of that bitter cup which the Father hath given me, and have glorified the Father in taking upon me the sins of the world, in the which I have suffered the will of the Father in all things from the beginning.

"And it came to pass that when Jesus had spoken these words the whole multitude fell to the earth; for they remembered that it had been prophesied among them that Christ should show himself unto them after his ascension into heaven.

"And it came to pass that the Lord spake unto them saying:

"Arise and come forth unto me, that ye may thrust your hands into my side, and also that ye may feel the prints of the nails in my hands and in my feet, that ye may know that I am the God of Israel, and the God of the whole earth, and have been slain for the sins of the world.

"And it came to pass that the multitude went forth, and thrust their hands into his side, and did feel the prints of the nails in his hands and in his feet; and this they did do, going forth one by one until they had all gone forth, and did see with their eyes and did feel with their hands, and did know of a surety and did bear record, that it was he, of whom it was written by the prophets, that should come.

"And when they had all gone forth and had witnessed for themselves, they did cry out with one accord, saying:

"Hosanna! Blessed be the name of the Most High God! And they did fall down at the feet of Jesus, and did worship him." (3 Nephi 11:1-17.)

Among the Nephites Christ labored for many days, blessing their children, healing their sick, raising some of the dead, and otherwise ministering as he did in Palestine.

All of this was after his resurrection. He was still a Person, a resurrected Being, with a physical body of flesh and bone. He was a great Reality; people could see him, hear him, feel his hands upon them. He ate before them, he wept, he prayed. Was this not a mighty revelation of the personality and nature of the Savior of the world? And since he told Philip "He that hath seen me hath seen the Father" (John 14:9), does not his Father possess those same characteristics?

Were not the Father and the Son separate Beings? For example, note this conversation as he met Mary following the resurrection:

"Jesus saith unto her, Mary. She turned herself, and saith unto him, Rabboni; which is to say, Master.

"Jesus saith unto her, Touch me not; for I am not yet ascended to my Father: but go to my brethren, and say unto them, I ascend unto my Father, and your Father; and to my God, and your God.

"Mary Magdalene came and told the disciples that she had

seen the Lord, and that he had spoken these things unto her." (John 20:16-18.)

The reality of his personal physical resurrection is provided in these words:

"And as they thus spake, Jesus himself stood in the midst of them, and saith unto them, Peace be unto you.

"But they were terrified and affrighted, and supposed that they had seen a spirit.

"And he said unto them, Why are ye troubled? and why do thoughts arise in your hearts?

"Behold my hands and my feet, that it is I myself: handle me, and see; for a spirit hath not flesh and bones, as ye see me have.

"And when he had thus spoken, he shewed them his hands and his feet.

"And while they yet believed not for joy, and wondered, he said unto them, Have ye here any meat?

"And they gave him a piece of a broiled fish, and of an honeycomb.

"And he took it, and did eat before them." (Luke 24:36-43.)

Doubting Thomas was given a physical demonstration of the reality of Christ as a Person in his resurrected form. It will be remembered that Thomas said:

"Except I shall see in his hands the print of the nails, and put my finger into the print of the nails, and thrust my hand into his side, I will not believe." (John 20:25.)

But then we have this:

"And after eight days again his disciples were within, and Thomas with them: then came Jesus, the doors being shut, and stood in the midst, and said, Peace be unto you.

"Then saith he to Thomas, Reach hither thy finger, and behold my hands; and reach hither thy hand, and thrust it into my side: and be not faithless, but believing.

"And Thomas answered and said unto him, My Lord and my God.

"Jesus saith unto him, Thomas, because thou hast seen me, thou hast believed: blessed are they that have not seen, and yet have believed." (John 20:26-29.)

Sectarianism had these scriptures all through the years, but never understood or believed them, so bound were they by tradition.

But Joseph Smith's revelations of God made the scriptures clear and in the light of modern revelation all these things became completely understandable. God is real. He is separate from his Beloved Son, just as any father and son are separate. They are both Persons, and man is made in their image.

Revelation to Joseph Smith concerning the creation of man made this concept more clear. We read:

"And I, God, said unto mine Only Begotten, which was with me from the beginning: Let us make man in our image, after our likeness; and it was so. And I, God, said: Let them have dominion over the fishes of the sea, and over the fowl of the air, and over the cattle, and over all the earth, and over every creeping thing that creepeth upon the earth.

"And I, God, created man in mine own image, in the image of mine Only Begotten created I him; male and female created I them." (Moses 2:26-27.)

To clarify it once and for all we have this from the writings and revelations of Joseph Smith:

"The Father has a body of flesh and bones as tangible as man's; the Son also; but the Holy Ghost has not a body of flesh and bones, but is a personage of Spirit. Were it not so, the Holy Ghost could not dwell in us." (D&C 130:22.)

So the basis for a genuine faith was restored through the Prophet Joseph Smith: the true knowledge of the nature of God.

Ten

Prophecy Restored

Could God direct his people and his Church unless he communicated with them? Obviously not. For this reason he placed in his Church inspired prophets to whom he spoke and through whom he communicated with the people.

All through the Old Testament period, prophets ministered among the people, and their writings are what make up the Old Testament.

But were there New Testament prophets also? Were prophets only for Old Testament times?

When Paul described the organization of the Christian Church, he said this:

"And he gave some, apostles; and some, prophets; and some, evangelists; and some, pastors and teachers;

"For the perfecting of the saints, for the work of the ministry, for the edifying of the body of Christ:

"Till we all come in the unity of the faith, and of the knowledge of the Son of God, unto a perfect man, unto the measure of the stature of the fulness of Christ:

"That we henceforth be no more children, tossed to and

fro, and carried about with every wind of doctrine, by the sleight of men, and cunning craftiness, whereby they lie in wait to deceive." (Ephesians 4:11-14.)

Prophets therefore were placed in the Christian Church as definite officers with special callings, as were the apostles, the evangelists, the pastors, and the teachers.

Their calling, described with the duties of these other officers, was "for the perfecting of the Saints, for the work of the ministry, for the edifying of the body of Christ."

Why for the "perfecting of the Saints"?

Because Christ had commanded that we become perfect— even as our Father in Heaven is perfect. (See Matthew 5:48.)

How could imperfect man hope to achieve such a goal? The Church was given as a means by which we may reach perfection, and the men who would teach this curriculum in perfection would be these apostles, prophets, evangelists, pastors, and teachers. And how would this be done?

Amos had said that God would do nothing except through his servants the prophets. So God would speak to them and direct them; and they in turn would direct the people.

Paul said these officers were for the edifying of the body of Christ. The body of Christ is defined by Paul himself as the membership of His Church. (See Ephesians 1:23; Colossians 1:18.)

Then inspired instruction was to be given by the prophets and apostles and their aides for the edification of Church members. That edification would help members to achieve this goal of eventually becoming perfect as their Father in Heaven.

This would mean continuous revelation. But that was no different from the way in which God dealt with the Old Testament peoples. From Adam to Malachi, he dealt through prophets.

Was the Lord to change his pattern in New Testament times? Of course not. Therefore, he placed prophets in his New Testament Church.

Part of this teaching by the prophets was to shield the members from false doctrine; hence, Paul said, explaining why these officers were needed: "That we henceforth be no more children, tossed to and fro, and carried about with every wind of doctrine, by the sleight of men, and cunning craftiness, whereby they lie in wait to deceive." (Ephesians 4:14.)

When Paul spoke of perfecting the Saints, he made it clear that these officers were required in the Lord's true Church:

"Till we all come in the unity of the faith, and of the knowledge of the Son of God, unto a perfect man, unto the measure of the stature of the fulness of Christ." (Ephesians 4:13.)

The prophets and apostles could not know how to "edify the body of Christ" except they themselves were taught; and their teachings would come from the Holy Ghost, whereby they were provided with revelation and inspiration for this work.

They would teach the people the true meaning of the scriptures too, so that they would not be led astray; for they were told that many false teachers would arise and deceive many.

The Savior said:

"Take heed that no man deceive you.

"For many shall come in my name saying, I am Christ; and shall deceive many.

"And many false prophets shall rise, and shall deceive many.

"And because iniquity shall abound, the love of many shall wax cold.

"Then if any man shall say unto you, Lo, here is Christ, or there; believe it not.

"For there shall arise false Christs, and false prophets, and shall shew great signs and wonders; insomuch that, if it were possible, they shall deceive the very elect." (Matthew 24:4-5, 11-12, 23-24.)

Jude wrote:

"Beloved, when I gave all diligence to write unto you of the common salvation, it was needful for me to write unto you, and exhort you that ye should earnestly contend for the faith which was once delivered unto the saints.

"For there are certain men crept in unawares, who were before of old ordained to this condemnation, ungodly men, turning the grace of our God into lasciviousness, and denying the only Lord God, and our Lord Jesus Christ." (Jude 3-4.)

Paul wrote to Titus as follows:

"For there are many unruly and vain talkers and deceivers, specially they of the circumcision:

"Whose mouths must be stopped, who subvert whole houses, teaching things which they ought not, for filthy lucre's sake.

"They profess that they know God; but in works they deny him, being abominable, and disobedient, and unto every good work reprobate." (Titus 1:10-11, 16.)

Peter wrote:

"But there were false prophets also among the people, even as there shall be false teachers among you, who privily shall bring in damnable heresies, even denying the Lord that bought them, and bring upon themselves swift destruction.

"And many shall follow their pernicious ways; by reason of whom the way of truth shall be evil spoken of.

"And through covetousness shall they with feigned words make merchandise of you: whose judgment now of a long time lingereth not, and their damnation slumbereth not." (2 Peter 2:1-3.)

Apostasy had already begun in Paul's own time as we see from his first letter to the Corinthians (chapter one) and from his epistle to the Galatians wherein he said:

"I marvel that ye are so soon removed from him that called you into the grace of Christ unto another gospel:

"Which is not another; but there be some that trouble you, and would pervert the gospel of Christ.

"But though we, or an angel from heaven, preach any other gospel unto you than that which we have preached unto you, let him be accursed." (Galatians 1:6-8.)

And then we have this from Paul:

"Take heed therefore unto yourselves, and to all the flock, over the which the Holy Ghost hath made you overseers, to feed the church of God, which he hath purchased with his own blood.

"For I know this, that after my departing shall grievous wolves enter in among you, not sparing the flock.

"Also of your own selves shall men arise, speaking perverse things, to draw away disciples after them.

"Therefore watch, and remember, that by the space of three years I ceased not to warn every one night and day with tears." (Acts 20:28-31.)

It is obvious that prophets were needed to properly teach and protect the members of the Church. It was not merely for the period in which Peter and Paul lived. It was "till we all come in the unity of the faith" (Ephesians 4:13), which has never yet been achieved.

Prophets disappeared from the early Christian Church. The last of whom there is any record is John the Beloved, who was not seen or heard of after about the year A.D. 110, when it is thought he was in Ephesus.

When the prophets were no longer among the people and revelation from heaven stopped, worldliness took over and darkness covered the earth.

But the gift of prophecy must always be in the true church. Therefore that gift, of necessity, would form an important part of the restoration of all things because, as the scripture says, it must include "all things which God hath spoken by the mouth of all his holy prophets since the world began." (Acts 3:21.)

Revelation and prophecy can hardly be separated. Joseph Smith was given many revelations; they are published to the world. But he also was given the specific appointment to the *office* of *prophet*, this by the Lord himself.

When the Church was organized, the Lord gave this revelation:

"Behold, there shall be a record kept among you; and in it thou shalt be called a seer, a translator, a prophet, an apostle of Jesus Christ, an elder of the church through the will of God the Father, and the grace of your Lord Jesus Christ.

"Being inspired of the Holy Ghost to lay the foundation thereof, and to build it up unto the most holy faith.

"Which church was organized and established in the year of your Lord eighteen hundred and thirty, in the fourth month, and on the sixth day of the month which is called April.

"Wherefore, meaning the church, thou shalt give heed unto all his words and commandments which he shall give unto you as he receiveth them, walking in all holiness before me;

"For his word ye shall receive, as if from mine own mouth, in all patience and faith.

"For by doing these things the gates of hell shall not prevail against you; yea, and the Lord God will disperse the powers of darkness from before you, and cause the heavens to shake for your good, and his name's glory.

"For thus saith the Lord God: Him have I inspired to move the cause of Zion in mighty power for good, and his diligence I know, and his prayers I have heard." (D&C 21:1-7.)

It is noted that not only was Joseph made a prophet, but likewise a seer, a translator, an apostle of the Lord Jesus Christ, and an elder of the newly organized Church, and that he was inspired by the Holy Ghost to "lay the foundation thereof and to build it up unto the most holy faith."

Paul told the Ephesians that there must be apostles as well as prophets in the Church.

In our day the Lord called twelve apostles (as he had done in former days) to serve with the Prophet Joseph Smith, likewise to edify and protect the Church and to teach its principles abroad.

Anciently after an apostle died, he was replaced. That was the case with Judas, who was succeeded by Matthias. Obviously, then, it was the intention of the Lord that vacancies in the Quorum of the Twelve be filled and the quorum be perpetuated.

It is recalled that James the brother of John was killed by Herod. Another vacancy, therefore, occurred. The record is not complete as to each appointment in succession, but we do know that Paul and Barnabas were both named apostles. (Acts 13: 1-4; 14:14.)

There would not be a quorum of thirteen or fourteen "Twelve Apostles." So each of these men must have filled a vacancy. It is also believed that James the brother of the Lord was an apostle. (Acts 12:17; 15:13; Galatians 1:19.)

In that day, however, apostasy became so rampant and persecution so severe that no further meetings of the Twelve as a quorum were possible; more and more of the Twelve were martyred, and eventually all but John were gone. He was banished to Patmos, and later was taken by the Lord. In this manner the Quorum of the Twelve disappeared in that day, as did the prophets. Hence there was no more revelation, and spiritual darkness took over.

The Prophet Joseph, ordained by angelic ministry, called twelve men to the apostleship in his day. When he realized that he would be martyred, he gave to each of the apostles the keys and powers which the angels had given him, thus providing a way by which those keys could be perpetuated for all time.

As each new apostle is chosen today he is given these same powers and keys that the angels gave to Joseph Smith.

On this point these observations are valuable:

On February 27, 1835, according to minutes kept by Oliver Cowdery, in answer to a question pertaining to the importance of the calling of the Twelve and the difference of that calling from other callings in the Church, the Prophet said:

"They are to hold the keys of this ministry, to unlock the door of the Kingdom of heaven unto all nations, and to preach the Gospel to every creature."

You will note his words: *"They are to hold the keys of this ministry."* (B.H. Roberts, ed., *History of The Church of Jesus Christ of Latter-day Saints*, 7 vols. [Salt Lake City: Deseret Book Company, 1970], vol. 2, page 200. Italics added. Hereafter cited as *DHC*.) Who but Joseph Smith could perform such an ordination?

In connection with the dedicatory services in the Kirtland Temple, the Prophet Joseph Smith, on March 27, 1836, wrote this in his own history:

"I then called upon the quorums and congregation of Saints to acknowledge the Twelve Apostles, who were present, as Prophets, Seers, Revelators, and special witnesses to all the nations of the earth, *holding the keys of the kingdom*, to unlock it, or cause it to be done, among them, and uphold them by their prayers, which they assented to by rising." (*DHC*, vol. 2, page 417. Italics added.)

On August 16, 1841, the Prophet Joseph addressed a conference of the Saints. The official documentary history of the Church, approved by the Prophet and included in his own writings, says of this address:

"President Joseph Smith now arriving, proceeded to state

to the conference at considerable length, the object of their present meeting, and in addition to what President Young had stated in the morning, said that the time had come *when the Twelve should be called upon to stand in their place next to the First Presidency*, and attend to the settling of emigrants and the business of the Church in the stakes, and assist *to bear off the kingdom victoriously to the nations.* . . . Moved, seconded, and carried, that the conference approve of the instructions of President Smith in relation to the Twelve and that they proceed accordingly to attend to the duties of their office." (*DHC*, vol. 4, page 403. Italics added.)

Heber C. Kimball said:

"As to the power and authority invested in brother Brigham, do I doubt it? Have I the least hesitation as to his calling as the President of this Church? No, no more than I have that God sits upon His throne. *He has the same authority that brother Joseph had.* That authority was in the Twelve, and since brother Joseph stepped behind the vail, brother Brigham is his lawful successor. I bear testimony of what brother Joseph said on the stand in Nauvoo, and I presume hundreds here can bear witness of the same. Said he: 'These men that are set here behind me here on this stand, I have conferred upon them all the power, Priesthood, and authority *that God ever conferred upon me.*' " (*Journal of Discourses*, Vol. 1, page 206. Italics added. Hereafter cited as *JD*.)

Wilford Woodruff said:

"The last speech that Joseph Smith ever made to the quorum of the Apostles was in a building in Nauvoo and it was such a speech as I have never heard from mortal man before or since. He was clothed upon with the spirit and power of God. His face was clear as amber. The room was filled as with consuming fire. He stood three hours upon his feet. Said he, 'You Apostles of the Lamb of God have been chosen to carry out the purposes of the Lord on the earth. Now I have received, as prophet, seer and revelator, standing at the head of this dispensation, every key, every ordinance, every principle, and every priesthood that belongs to the last dispensation and fulness of times. *And I have sealed all these things upon your heads.*" (*Conference Report*, April 1898, page 89. Italics added.)

Brigham Young in a letter written to Orson Spencer on January 23, 1848, said:

"Joseph told the Twelve the year before he died, 'there is not one key or power to be bestowed on this church to lead the people into the celestial gate but *I have given you*, showed you, and talked it over to you; the kingdom is set up, and you have the perfect pattern, and you can go and build up the kingdom, and go in at the celestial gate, taking your train with you.' " (*Millennial Star*, 10:115. Italics added.)

Heber C. Kimball said:

"Bro. Joseph has passed behind the vail and he pulled off his shoes, and some one else puts them on, until he passes the vail to Bro. Joseph. President Young is our president, and our head, and he puts the shoes on first. . . . *The Twelve have received the keys of the kingdom and as long as there is one of them left, he will hold them in preference to any one else.*" (*Times and Seasons*, 5:664. Italics added.)

Orson Hyde said:

"The shafts of the enemy are always aimed at the head first. —Brother Joseph said some time before he was murdered, 'If I am taken away, upon you, the Twelve, will rest the responsibility of leading this people, and do not be bluffed off by any man.' . . . 'Now if they kill me *you have got all the keys, and all the ordinances and you can confer them upon others*, and the hosts of Satan will not be able to tear down the kingdom, as fast as you will be able to build it up; And . . . on your shoulders will the responsibility of leading this people rest, for the Lord is going to let me rest a while.' " (*Times and Seasons*, 5:650-651. Italics added.)

Orson Hyde further said:

"I will give you my testimony. In one particular place, in the presence of about sixty men, he [the Prophet Joseph] said, 'My work is about done; I am going to step aside a while. I am going to rest from my labors; for I have borne the [burden] and heat of the day, and now I am going to step aside and rest a little. And I roll the [burden] off my shoulders on the shoulders of the Twelve Apostles. Now, . . . round up your shoulders and bear off this kingdom.' " (*JD*, Vol. 13, page 180.)

Brigham Young said:

"I know there are those in our midst who will seek the lives of the Twelve as they did the lives of Joseph and Hyrum. We shall ordain others and give the fulness of the priesthood, so that if we are killed the fulness of the priesthood may remain.

"Joseph conferred upon our heads all the keys and powers belonging to the Apostleship which he himself held before he was taken away, and no man or set of men can get between Joseph and the Twelve in this world or in the world to come.

"How often has Joseph said to the Twelve, 'I have laid the foundation and you must build thereon, for upon your shoulders the kingdom rests.' " (*DHC*, vol. 7, page 230. Italics added.)

The right to exercise the sealing powers as restored through Elijah the prophet is reserved for the President of the Church himself and to those to whom he personally delegates that privilege.

With reference to this, Parley P. Pratt said:

"He proceeded to confer on elder Young, the President of the Twelve, the keys of the sealing power, as conferred in the last days by the spirit and power of Elijah, in order to seal the hearts of the fathers to the children and the hearts of the children to the fathers, lest the whole earth should be smitten with a curse." (*Millennial Star*, 5:151.)

On Monday, July 2, 1839, the Prophet met with the Twelve and other officers of the Church, and gave them instructions. He placed a synopsis of his own remarks in his journal, from which the following is copied:

"O ye Twelve! and all Saints! profit by this important *Key*—that in all your trials, troubles, temptations, afflictions, bonds, imprisonments and death, see to it, that you do not betray heaven; that you do not betray Jesus Christ; that you do not betray the brethren; that you do not betray the revelations of God, whether in the Bible, Book of Mormon, or Doctrine and Covenants, or any other that ever was or ever will be given and revealed unto man in this world or that which is to come. Yea, in all your kicking and flounderings, see to it that you do not this thing, lest innocent blood be found upon your skirts, and you go down to hell. All other sins are not to be compared to sinning against the Holy Ghost, *and proving a traitor to the brethren.*

"I will give you one of the *Keys* of the mysteries of the Kingdom. It is an eternal principle, that has existed with God from all eternity: That man who rises up to condemn others, finding fault with the Church, saying that they are out of the way, while he himself is righteous, then know assuredly, that that man is in the high road to apostasy; and if he does not repent, will apostatize, as God lives. The principle is as correct as the one that Jesus put forth in saying that he who seeketh a sign is an adulterous person; and that principle is eternal, undeviating, and firm as the pillars of heaven." (*DHC*, vol. 3, page 385. Some italics added.)

The right of the President to receive revelations for the Church is made clear as follows:

"But, behold, verily, verily, I say unto thee, no one shall be appointed to receive commandments and revelations in this church excepting my servant Joseph Smith, Jun., for he receiveth them even as Moses.

"For I have given unto him the keys of the mysteries, and the revelations which are sealed, until I shall appoint unto them another in his stead." (D&C 28:2, 7.)

"For behold, verily, verily, I say unto you, that ye have received a commandment for a law unto my church, through him whom I have appointed unto you to receive commandments and revelations from my hand.

"And this ye shall know assuredly—that there is none other appointed unto you to receive commandments and revelations until he be taken, if he abide in me.

"But verily, verily, I say unto you, that none else shall be appointed unto this gift except it be through him; for if it be taken from him he shall not have power except to appoint another in his stead.

"And this shall be a law unto you, that ye receive not the teachings of any that shall come before you as revelations or commandments;

"And this I give unto you that you may not be deceived, that you may know they are not of me.

"For verily I say unto you, that he that is ordained of me shall come in at the gate and be ordained as I have told you before, to teach those revelations which you have received and shall receive through him whom I have appointed." (D&C 43:2-7.)

So the apostleship and all its keys were restored in this dispensation; and since that restoration, each new apostle has been given the keys as part of his ordination. The appointment and administration of these officers constitute an infallible mark of identification of the true Church of Jesus Christ.

The restoration of these powers was vital to the preparation needed for the second coming of the Savior. How could the foundation for his coming be laid without divine authority? Since it was not on earth, how could mankind again obtain it? Only by restoration. And this was done!

Eleven

For the Ministry

When Paul described the organization of the true Church to the Ephesians, he pointedly said that the purpose of appointing prophets and apostles was for the "work of the ministry," as well as for the perfection and edification of the Saints. (See Ephesians 4:11-14.)

How were they involved in the "work of the ministry"? Was it that they were traveling ministers for Christ, preaching his word wherever they went? Yes, by all means. But there was more.

How were these ministers for Christ to be called? That is a vital question; and the correct answer becomes another mark of identification of the true Church.

The Old Testament Prophet Amos had said:

"Surely the Lord God will do nothing, but he revealeth his secret unto his servants the prophets." (Amos 3:7.) This is one of the most significant passages in all holy writ. Why? Because it gets down to the basic operation of the Lord's Church and sets forth an indispensable principle.

God works through his divinely appointed prophets. He

will do *nothing* without revealing his purposes to them. That means he will not carry on his ministry without them.

If he will do nothing except through his prophets, he will not appoint men to the priesthood or to the ministry without prophets. This comes down to the fundamental question of divine authority among men. How is it obtained?

According to Amos, it must be through the ministry of prophets; and according to Paul, those appointments are "for the work of the ministry." Then the work of the ministry is directly associated with the call of the prophets themselves and also with the calls they issue to others as directed by the Lord.

When Paul wrote to the Hebrews he gave further explanation. He described the process by which men receive the priesthood and said: "No man taketh this honour unto himself, but he that is called of God, as was Aaron." (Hebrews 5:4.)

Think of the significance of that declaration! Men must be called, as was Aaron, to enter the ministry.

Immediately we ask how Aaron was called. We read the details in Exodus, chapter 28. God in heaven spoke to his living prophet Moses on earth and directed that prophet to call Aaron and his sons to the ministry.

"And take thou unto thee Aaron thy brother, and his sons with him, from among the children of Israel, that he may minister unto me in the priest's office."

Other translations of the Bible all agree. For example, the Knox Roman Catholic Bible reads on this point: "And now, that I may have priests to serve me among the sons of Israel, summon thy brother Aaron, with his sons, Nadab, Abju, Eleazar and Ithmar."

The fortieth chapter of Exodus goes into further detail.

When Aaron died, the same procedure was followed. It was the pattern God gave to Israel. We read:

"Take Aaron and Eleazar his son, and bring them up unto the mount Hor:

"And strip Aaron of his garments and put them upon Eleazar his son: and Aaron shall be gathered unto his people, and shall die there.

"And Moses did as the Lord commanded." (Numbers 20:25-27.)

In the same manner Joshua was called to be the successor to Moses. The scripture reads:

"Now after the death of Moses the servant of the Lord it came to pass, that the Lord spake unto Joshua the son of Nun, Moses' minister, saying,

"Moses my servant is dead; now therefore arise, go over this Jordan, thou, and all this people, unto the land which I do give to them, even to the children of Israel.

"Every place that the sole of your foot shall tread upon, that have I given unto you, as I said unto Moses." (Joshua 1:1-3.)

It also reads:

"And Joshua the son of Nun was full of the spirit of wisdom; for Moses had laid his hands upon him; and the children of Israel hearkened unto him, and did as the Lord commanded Moses." (Deuteronomy 34:9.)

But more specifically we have this:

"And the Lord said unto Moses, Take thee Joshua the son of Nun, a man in whom is the spirit, and lay thine hand upon him;

"And set him before Eleazar the priest, and before all the congregation; and give him a charge in their sight.

"And thou shalt put some of thine honour upon him, that all the congregation of the children of Israel may be obedient.

"And he shall stand before Eleazar the priest, who shall ask counsel for him after the judgment of Urim before the Lord: at his word shall they go out, and at his word they shall come in, both he, and all the children of Israel with him, even all the congregation.

"And Moses did as the Lord commanded him: and he took Joshua, and set him before Eleazar the priest, and before all the congregation:

"And he laid his hands upon him, and gave him a charge, as the Lord commanded by the hand of Moses." (Numbers 27:18-23.)

Was this pattern followed in New Testament times also? Note the call of Paul and Barnabas:

"Now there were in the church that was at Antioch certain prophets and teachers; as Barnabas, and Simeon that was called

Niger, and Lucius of Cyrene, and Manaen, which had been brought up with Herod the tetrarch, and Saul.

"As they ministered to the Lord, and fasted, the Holy Ghost said, Separate me Barnabas and Saul for the work whereunto I have called them.

"And when they had fasted and prayed, and laid their hands on them, they sent them away.

"So they, being sent forth by the Holy Ghost, departed unto Seleucia; and from thence they sailed to Cyprus.

"And when they were at Salamis, they preached the word of God in the synagogues of the Jews: and they had also John to their minister." (Acts 13:1-5.)

The Roman Catholic Bible of 1947, published in Great Britain, reads on this point:

"Separate me Saul and Barnabas for the work whereunto I have taken them, Then they, fasting and praying, and *imposing their hands upon them*, sent them away." (Italics added.)

The Authentic New Testament by Schonfield reads: "The Holy Spirit said, Set apart for us Barnabas and Saul for the task I have assigned them."

The New English Bible says:

"Set Barnabas and Saul apart for me to do the work to which I have called them."

The Revised Version of the Bible (Protestant) reads:

"The Holy Spirit said: 'Set apart for me Barnabas and Saul for the work to which I have called them.' "

In each instance these various Bibles also indicate that the power was transmitted by the laying on of hands. Thus were the men "set apart" even as they are set apart today. For example, the Goodspeed American translation says: "So after fasting and prayer, they laid their hands upon them and let them go."

The ancient apostles were prophets also, and hence sought and obtained the Lord's direction in calling Matthias to succeed Judas. Again, it was direct revelation to the living prophets through whom the new officer was chosen.

Another instance of prophecy being involved in the call to the ministry appears in the case of Timothy. He was duly ordained to the work (see 1 Timothy 2:7), and Paul then reminds him not to neglect that ordination *"which was given thee by prophecy, with the laying on of the hands. . . ."* (1 Timothy 4:14. Italics added.)

The apostles themselves were ordained by the Christ (see Matthew 10:1; Mark 3:14; John 15:16). Likewise the Seventy. (See Luke 10:1.)

Regarding the choosing of the seven assistants to the Twelve, the scripture says: "Whom they set before the apostles: and when they had prayed, they laid their hands on them." (Acts 6:6.)

Prophecy ceased to exist in early Christianity. Many Christian denominations therefore held that apostles and prophets were no longer needed and that the Bible contained all the necessary direction from heaven.

But the Christians split into numerous denominations. Why? Because prophecy ceased—God was no longer directing his Church—the Church of Jesus Christ was no longer on the earth. Confusion reigned.

Ministers became the products of colleges and seminaries and received both their instruction *and their authority* from those colleges. But the colleges admitted and taught that there were no more prophets. The men they appointed to the ministry obviously were not called of God as was Aaron. The only authority they had was that of the college from which they graduated; and it was man's authority, not God's.

Other men have started preaching because they felt an inward urge to do so. They were self-appointed, and hence had no divine authority either. Where was their laying on of hands?

Then could they properly officiate in the ordinances of Christ? Of course not. They were not called of God and held no divine authority. That meant that even though they performed ordinances, their actions were meaningless because they acted without a divine appointment.

Jesus said that when we attempt to worship by the direction of men, our worship is in vain. (See Matthew 15:9.) On this point it is interesting to read the Jerusalem Bible's rendering (Roman Catholic):

"This people honors me only with lip service, while their

hearts are far from me. *The worship they offer me is worthless*: the doctrines they teach are only human regulations." (Mark 7:6-9. Italics added.)

Also on this point it is interesting to see how Dr. Schonfield translates Matthew 7:2-23 in the Authentic New Testament. His version reads:

"Many will say unto me at that time, Master, Master, have we not prophesied in thy name and in thy name performed many miracles? But then I shall tell them plainly: *I have never authorized you. Be off with you, you illegal practitioners.*" (Italics added.)

Divine authority is required for anyone to act in His holy name. Since men must be called by revelation through the Lord's prophet, the work of the ministry cannot proceed without prophets.

The institution of prophecy and revelation is another of the vital factors in the true Church as restored through the Prophet Joseph Smith. It is an unmistakable mark of identification by which we may know that The Church of Jesus Christ of Latter-day Saints is true.

The restoration of the principle of prophecy and the resumption of current revelation through the living prophets are two primary means by which the way is being prepared for the second coming of Christ.

Through this institution, again it is seen how Joseph Smith was a forerunner who prepared the way for the Lord's return.

Twelve

Additional Scripture

Another of the infallible signs of the true Church is that it will produce new additional scripture.

For centuries the various denominations have taught that there is no need for current revelation, no need of prophets, seers, or revelators, and that the Bible contains the full measure of the word of God.

When mention is made of additional scripture, some immediately point to the verses in the last chapter of the book of Revelation which say that there should be no additions to that book and that people who add to or subtract from it will be cursed. (See Revelation 22:18-19.)

They do not know that John was speaking only of the *book of Revelation* when he wrote those words. He could not possibly have referred to the whole Bible, for the Bible at that time had not been compiled. Actually John's gospel was written after the book of Revelation.

John himself makes clear what book is meant:

"Blessed is he that readeth, and they that hear the words of *this prophecy*, and keep those things which are written therein."

And: "What thou seest, *write in a book*." (Revelation 1:3, 11. Italics added.)

So it is the book of this prophecy to which the last few verses of the book of Revelation refer, not to any other. If it were all-encompassing, we would have to eliminate John's gospel (for one thing). Who would want that?

Also, the Bible as such was not compiled for several centuries *after* John's revelation, and therefore was not yet in book form. Hence, his words could not refer to the entire Bible by any means.

It is interesting to note that references are recorded in Deuteronomy 4:2 and 12:32 in which Moses gives instructions very much like those of John. If we were to place upon the verses in Deuteronomy the same interpretation that some put upon those similar words in Revelation, it would mean the elimination of the entire Old Testament from Moses on and also the whole New Testament. Obviously, that sort of interpretation is entirely wrong.

What are the facts with regard to additional scripture? To get the key to this matter, let us examine the manner in which we obtained the Bible. It was not all written at the same time.

The five books of Moses came first. We know that Moses wrote them, for the Lord made it known to the Prophet Joseph Smith. Our book of Moses in the Pearl of Great Price makes this clear. There the Genesis account is given in greater detail than we have it in the Bible, and there also is the revelation of the Lord that these were God's words to Moses. Otherwise Moses could not have written about the Creation, the Flood, and the early patriarchs. The Lord gave both Moses and Joseph Smith this information by revelation.

Moses wrote up to the time of his death. Then of course someone else closed the record. (See 1 Nephi 5:11-14; 3 Nephi 15.)

But would the Bible stop there, or would more be added? More was added, as we know from the text itself.

Joshua succeeded Moses in the leadership of Israel. Joshua was a prophet. God spoke to him. Note the commission the Lord gave to him. Moses had died and Joshua was now called:

"So Moses the servant of the Lord died there in the land of Moab, according to the word of the Lord.

"And he buried him in a valley in the land of Moab, over against Bethpeor: but no man knoweth of his sepulchre unto this day.

"And Moses was an hundred and twenty years old when he died: his eye was not dim, nor his natural force abated.

"And the children of Israel wept for Moses in the plains of Moab thirty days: so the days of weeping and mourning for Moses were ended.

"And Joshua the son of Nun was full of the spirit of wisdom; for Moses had laid his hands upon him: and the children of Israel hearkened unto him, and did as the Lord commanded Moses." (Deuteronomy 34:5-9.)

After Moses' death the Lord spoke to Joshua as follows:

"Now after the death of Moses the servant of the Lord it came to pass, that the Lord spake unto Joshua the son of Nun, Moses' minister, saying,

"Moses my servant is dead; now therefore arise, go over this Jordan, thou, and all this people, unto the land which I do give to them, even to the children of Israel.

"Every place that the sole of your foot shall tread upon, that have I given unto you, as I said unto Moses.

"From the wilderness and this Lebanon even unto the great river, the river Euphrates, all the land of the Hittites, and unto the great sea toward the going down of the sun, shall be your coast.

"There shall not any man be able to stand before thee all the days of thy life: as I was with Moses, so I will be with thee: I will not fail thee, nor forsake thee.

"Be strong and of a good courage: for unto this people shalt thou divide for an inheritance the land, which I sware unto their fathers to give them.

"Only be thou strong and very courageous, that thou mayest observe to do according to all the law, which Moses my servant commanded thee: turn not from it to the right hand or to the left, that thou mayest prosper whithersoever thou goest.

"This book of the law shall not depart out of thy mouth;

but thou shalt meditate therein day and night, that thou mayest observe to do according to all that is written therein: for then thou shalt make thy way prosperous, and then thou shalt have good success.

"Have not I commanded thee? Be strong and of a good courage; be not afraid, neither be thou dismayed: for the Lord thy God is with thee whithersoever thou goest." (Joshua 1:1-9.)

Here we see the beginning of a pattern with respect to the scriptures. The Lord "will do nothing, but he revealeth his secret unto his servants the prophets." (Amos 3:7.) He had to direct his people by revelation. Revelation came through the prophets, and their writings became scripture.

Each record was added to the previously prepared books of scripture and hence became new and additional scripture itself.

It was so with Joshua and his book. Following Joshua came the Judges. The history of Israel during their regime was recorded, and *added to the existing volume of scripture.*

The Prophet Samuel was called. Two books of the Bible contain the record of his ministry. They were added to the existing volume of scripture, and thus they became new and additional scripture.

We have the two books of Kings. It is not known with any certainty who wrote those books. But they were sacred histories of that period of Israel's activities and became scripture as they were added to the already existing books.

The books of Chronicles were added similarly and were accepted as scripture.

When the Prophet Ezra arose, his record was likewise added, as was the case with the writings or histories of all the other Old Testament prophets including Isaiah, Jeremiah, Ezekiel, Malachi and Micah.

As each new prophet arose and carried on his ministry, his history became an addition to the growing volume of scripture. That is the way we obtained the entire Old Testament. It was a growing thing. It could not have been done unless God had living prophets among his people over the centuries. It was part and parcel of God's plan. Without revelation there would be no divine direction. Without it, people always go astray.

Just as the Apostle John was commanded to write his revelations, the other prophets also were commanded to write theirs. (See Exodus 17:14; 24:4-12; 34:27; Joshua 24:26; 1 Samuel 10:25; Nehemiah 9:38; Isaiah 8:1; 30:8; Jeremiah 30:2; 31:33; 36:2; Ezekiel 37:16; Habakkuk 2:2.)

The writings of each in their turn were added to the existing volume of holy writ and became part of it. That is the way we obtained our Bible. There was no other way. The entire book did not come at once as if by magic. It was an ongoing, growing thing, developing out of the ministries of the prophets over the centuries.

To say that scripture is not a growing thing is to ignore the facts.

Does this pattern also apply to the New Testament? Of course it does. How else would we have obtained the writings of Matthew, Mark, Luke, and John, of Paul and Peter, of James and Jude? Each wrote as a prophet. Their books were the inspired Word of God. But they followed the pattern. Scripture consists of the writings and histories of the prophets.

And God placed prophets in ancient Israel from Moses to Malachi, and also installed prophets in the Christian Church as it was organized. (Ephesians 2:19-21; 4:11-16; Acts 13:1-4.)

All of this adds up to one important fact: One of the infallible marks of identification by which we may recognize the true Church is that it will produce new and additional scripture. Again, this is by reason of the ministry of the prophets within it.

If there are no prophets, can any denomination claim to be the true Church of Christ? Without prophets there is neither divine direction nor *divine acknowledgment*, nor is there any divine authority by which to carry on the ministry.

Did not Paul make it clear that all ministers for Christ must be called of God as was Aaron? (See Hebrews 5:4.) And was not Aaron called by direct revelation to a living prophet? (See Exodus 28.)

If a church does not have true prophets, neither can it produce new and additional scripture.

It is no wonder that the Apostle Peter declared that before the second coming of Christ there would have to be a restoration of all things spoken of by all the holy prophets from the beginning of the world. (See Acts 3.)

The principle of revelation with the ministry of apostles and prophets of necessity would have to be a part of that restoration. And so it was.

Joseph Smith was raised up as the modern prophet of God. The Lord talked with him face to face repeatedly. Joseph received the ministration of angels and was given divine authority by those angels.

But what about new scripture? Does this Church produce new scripture? Indeed it has done so already and will continue to do so.

In The Church of Jesus Christ of Latter-day Saints resides the gift of revelation and prophecy. Prophets lead the way. They are inspired men of God.

The first of our new scripture is the Book of Mormon, brought to light by angelic power, translated by revelation from God, and published to the world. It is the sacred history of ancient America, as the Bible is the sacred record of Palestine.

We have the Doctrine and Covenants, a compilation of many of the revelations of the Lord to the Prophet Joseph Smith. We have the Pearl of Great Price which contains additional inspired and sacred writings. And, of course, we accept the Bible as the Word of God.

Four volumes of scripture. Three of them new. All three produced on the same basis as the Bible, following the same sacred pattern.

They point precisely and accurately to The Church of Jesus Christ of Latter-day Saints as the true Church of God, set up, nourished and developed by the Almighty himself.

And what about the record of the present-day apostles? Their ministries are being recorded day by day by the historians of the Church as carefully as Luke recorded the acts of the apostles in ancient times.

Which church is right? This important mark of identification affirms that this Church is God's own and that Joseph Smith, through whom it all came to pass, is verily His true Prophet.

Again, new scripture was part of the preparation for the second coming of the Lord, and Joseph Smith was the instrument through whom new scripture was given to us. Like John, he prepared the way.

Thirteen

Symbols of the Atonement

Christ gave us two symbols of his holy atonement. Most people use the sign of the cross and declare it to be the true symbol of Christianity. But it is not so. The cross is but a symbol of the brutal form of execution used by the Romans.

The true symbols of the crucifixion and resurrection of the Savior are:

1.   The sacrament of the Lord's Supper, given in remembrance of his torn flesh and his blood which was shed on the cross.

2.   And baptism by immersion, as a symbol of his burial in the tomb and his subsequent resurrection.

When the Savior sat with his disciples at the Last Supper, he broke bread and gave it to them to eat and said: "Take, eat; this is my body." (Matthew 26:26.)

Then, giving them the cup, he said, "Drink ye all of it, for this is my blood of the new testament which is shed for many for the remission of sins." (Matthew 26:27-28.)

Many misunderstandings have resulted from these words.

It is not difficult, however, to determine the meaning of

what the Lord said. The references given above are from the King James translation of the Bible.

Some of the newer versions make it more clear. For example, Moffatt's translation of Luke 22:19-21 says: "Then he took a loaf and after thanking God he broke it and gave it to them, saying *this means my body* given up for your sake. Do this in memory of me." (Italics added.)

When Moffatt translated 1 Corinthians 11:23-29, he used the same expression, indicating that both passages had the same meaning. Here again he said: "The Lord Jesus took a loaf and after thanking God he broke it, saying, *this means my body*, broken for you. Do this in memory of me." (Italics added.)

When Schonfield translated Mark 14:22, he wrote:

"He took the bread and reciting the blessing, broke it, and gave it to them and said: Take it. *It signifies my body*."

In his translation of 1 Corinthians 11:24, he said again: "This *signifies my body*, broken in your behalf. Do this in commemoration of me." (Italics added.)

The New World Translation of Luke 22:19 reads: "He took a loaf, gave thanks, broke it and gave it to them, saying, *this means my body* which is to be given in your behalf. Keep doing this in remembrance of me." (Italics added.)

Referring to the cup, Moffatt says in Luke 22:19-21: "In the same way he took the cup after supper saying, *this cup means the new covenant* ratified by my blood; as often as you drink it, do it in memory of me." (Italics added.)

Schonfield in his Authentic New Testament has the reference in Matthew saying "This *signifies* my blood of the covenant poured out for many in forgiveness of sins."

His version of Mark says: "It *signifies* my blood of the covenant poured out for many." In his translation of the passage in 1 Corinthians he says: "This cup *signifies* the new covenant in my blood." (Italics added.)

The Revised Standard Version on 1 Corinthians 11 says: "*This cup is the new covenant* in my blood." (Italics added.)

The New English Bible for the same verse says: "*This cup is the new covenant* sealed by my blood." (Italics added.)

Philips has the same verse read: "*This cup is the new agree-*

ment in my blood." The Philips version of Luke 22:22 reads: *"This cup is the new agreement* made in my own blood which is shed for you." (Italics added.)

The New World Translation of the Luke 22 passage: "Also the cup in the same way, after they had the evening meal, saying, *This cup means the new covenant by virtue of my blood* which is to be poured out in your behalf." (Italics added.)

It is interesting that all the new versions clarify these things:

1.   The bread is to be broken to represent his broken flesh as a symbol. A bakery wafer, whole and fresh and unbroken, hardly fits the subject.

2.   The bread *signifies* his broken flesh, or it is a symbol of his broken flesh. None of the new translations in any way whatever support the idea of transubstantiation, which teaches that it is the literal flesh of Christ.

3.   The drinking from the cup again *signifies* his blood, or *it is a sign of a new agreement* made between the Christ and the individual who partakes. It is the sign of a covenant, a pledge to always remember him. It is by partaking of it that we seal the covenant. The doctrine of transubstantiation here again does not appear. We do not drink of Christ's actual blood, reproduced each time the sacrament is served. We drink in remembrance of his blood and thereby enter into covenant with him.

This entire ordinance of the Last Supper is symbolic so far as the emblems are concerned. But partaking of those emblems places us under covenant with God to remember the Christ and to serve him.

This is made abundantly clear in the sacramental prayers given us through the Prophet Joseph Smith (see D&C 20:77-79) and in the Book of Mormon (see Moroni 4, 5). When the Savior provided the sacrament for the Nephites, he said:

"And when the multitude had eaten and were filled, he said unto the disciples: Behold there shall one be ordained among you, and to him will I give power that he shall break bread and bless it and give it unto the people of my church, unto all those who shall believe and be baptized in my name.

"And this shall ye always observe to do, even as I have done, even as I have broken bread and blessed it and given it unto you.

"And this shall ye do in remembrance of my body, which I have shown unto you. And it shall be a testimony unto the Father that ye do always remember me. And if ye do always remember me ye shall have my Spirit to be with you." (3 Nephi 18:5-7.)

As he gave them the cup he also said: "Ye shall do it in remembrance of my blood, which I have shed for you, that you may witness unto the Father that ye do always remember me." (3 Nephi 18:11.)

So the sacrament of the Lord's Supper was the divinely given symbol of the Crucifixion, of the death and suffering of the Lord whose body was torn and bruised on Calvary.

What is the purpose of the other symbol? It is to remind us of the other portion of the Atonement, his burial and resurrection, teaching us that not only was he resurrected but that we will be likewise.

Immersion baptism alone can provide that symbolism. We are buried in the water as Jesus was buried in the tomb; and we are brought forth from this watery grave as Christ came forth physically from his grave. He came forth to a newness of life—in the resurrection. We are brought forth from the water in a newness of life—in the Church, cleansed from sin. (See Romans 6:4-5; Colossians 2:12, 3:1.)

Dr. James E. Talmage in his book *The Articles of Faith* describes the symbolism in baptism as follows:

"The symbolism of the Baptismal Rite is preserved in no form other than immersion. The Savior compared baptism to a birth, and declared such to be essential to the life that leads to the kingdom of God. None can say that a birth is typified by a sprinkling of water upon the face. Not the least of the distinctions that have contributed to Christ's preeminence as a teacher of teachers consists in His precise and forceful use of language; His comparisons and metaphors are always expressive, His parables convincing; and so inappropriate a similitude as is implied in such a misrepresentation of birth would be entirely foreign to the Lord's methods.

"Baptism has also been very impressively compared to a burial, followed by a resurrection; and in this symbol of the bodily death and resurrection of His Son has God promised to grant remission of sins. In writing to the Romans, Paul says: 'Know ye not, that so many of us as were baptized into Jesus Christ were baptized into his death? Therefore we are buried with him by baptism into death: that like as Christ was raised up from the dead by the glory of the Father, even so we also should walk in newness of life. For if we have been planted together in the likeness of his death, we shall be also in the likeness of his resurrection.' And again, the same apostle writes: 'Buried with him in baptism, wherein also ye are risen with him through the faith of the operation of God, who hath raised him from the dead.' Among all the varied forms of baptism practised by man, immersion alone typifies a birth marking the beginning of a new career, or the sleep of the grave with subsequent victory over death." (12th ed. [Salt Lake City: The Church of Jesus Christ of Latter-day Saints, 1916], pages 138-139.)

The true sacrament of the Lord's Supper and the true baptism were restored through the Prophet Joseph Smith, another part of the preparation for the second coming of Christ.

Fourteen

The Truth About Baptism

Baptism in water is a vital part of the gospel of the Lord Jesus Christ.

It is required of all who are of the age of accountability. Infant baptism is not of God. Baptism is for repentant sinners, for therein do they obtain a remission of their sins.

It was the Prophet Joseph Smith who gave to the earth through the inspiration of heaven a true understanding of baptism.

Is baptism necessary? The Book of Mormon gives us this:

"And he commanded them that there should be no contention one with another, but that they should look forward with one eye, having one faith and one baptism, having their hearts knit together in unity and in love one towards another." (Mosiah 18:21.)

"And now, if the Lamb of God, he being holy, should have need to be baptized by water, to fulfil all righteousness, O then, how much more need have we, being unholy, to be baptized, yea, even by water!

"And now, I would ask of you, my beloved brethren,

wherein the Lamb of God did fulfil all righteousness in being baptized by water?

"Know ye not that he was holy? But notwithstanding he being holy, he showeth unto the children of men that, according to the flesh he humbleth himself before the Father, and witnesseth unto the Father that he would be obedient unto him in keeping his commandments."

"And the Father said: Repent ye, repent ye, and be baptized in the name of my Beloved Son.

"And also, the voice of the Son came unto me, saying: He that is baptized in my name, to him will the Father give the Holy Ghost, like unto me; wherefore, follow me, and do the things which ye have seen me do." (2 Nephi 31:5-7, 11-12.)

"And he commandeth all men that they must repent, and be baptized in his name, having perfect faith in the Holy One of Israel, or they cannot be saved in the kingdom of God." (2 Nephi 9:23.)

As to the mode of baptism, the Lord taught this:

"And Nephi arose and went forth, and bowed himself before the Lord and did kiss his feet.

"And the Lord commanded him that he should arise. And he arose and stood before him.

"And the Lord said unto him: I give unto you power that ye shall baptize this people when I am again ascended into heaven.

"And again the Lord called others, and said unto them likewise; and he gave unto them power to baptize. And he said unto them: On this wise shall ye baptize; and there shall be no disputations among you.

"Verily I say unto you, that whoso repenteth of his sins through your words and desireth to be baptized in my name, on this wise shall ye baptize them—Behold, ye shall go down and stand in the water, and in my name shall ye baptize them.

"And now behold, these are the words which ye shall say, calling them by name, saying:

"Having authority given me of Jesus Christ, I baptize you in the name of the Father, and of the Son, and of the Holy Ghost. Amen.

"And then shall ye immerse them in the water, and come forth again out of the water.

"And after this manner shall ye baptize in my name; for behold, verily I say unto you, that the Father, and the Son, and the Holy Ghost are one; and I am in the Father, and the Father in me, and the Father and I are one." (3 Nephi 11:19-27.)

And then the Savior added:

"And whoso believeth in me, and is baptized, the same shall be saved; and they are they who shall inherit the kingdom of God.

"And whoso believeth not in me, and is not baptized, shall be damned.

"Verily, verily, I say unto you, that this is my doctrine, and I bear record of it from the Father; and whoso believeth in me believeth in the Father also; and unto him will the Father bear record of me, for he will visit him with fire and with the Holy Ghost.

"And thus will the Father bear record of me, and the Holy Ghost will bear record unto him of the Father and me; for the Father, and I, and the Holy Ghost are one.

"And again I say unto you, ye must repent, and become as a little child, and be baptized in my name, or ye can in nowise receive these things.

"And again I say unto you, ye must repent, and be baptized in my name, and become as a little child, or ye can in nowise inherit the kingdom of God.

"Verily, verily, I say unto you, that this is my doctrine, and whoso buildeth upon this buildeth upon my rock, and the gates of hell shall not prevail against them." (3 Nephi 11:33-39.)

Of course this ordinance must be performed by one having divine authority; for as Paul said, "No man taketh this honour unto himself, but he that is called of God, as was Aaron." (Hebrews 5:4.)

Baptism of infants is prohibited by the Lord. The Book of Mormon explains in this language:

"Listen to the words of Christ, your Redeemer, your Lord and your God. Behold, I came into the world not to call the righteous but sinners to repentance; the whole need no physician, but they that are sick; wherefore, little children are whole, for they are not capable of committing sin; wherefore the curse of Adam is taken from them in me, that it hath no power over them; and the law of circumcision is done away in me.

"And after this manner did the Holy Ghost manifest the word of God unto me; wherefore, my beloved son, I know that it is solemn mockery before God, that ye should baptize little children.

"Behold I say unto you that this thing shall ye teach—repentance and baptism unto those who are accountable and capable of committing sin; yea, teach parents that they must repent and be baptized, and humble themselves as their little children, and they shall all be saved with their little children.

"And their little children need no repentance, neither baptism. Behold, baptism is unto repentance to the fulfilling the commandments unto the remission of sins.

"But little children are alive in Christ, even from the foundation of the world; if not so, God is a partial God, and also a changeable God, and a respecter of persons; for how many little children have died without baptism!

"Wherefore, if little children could not be saved without baptism, these must have gone to an endless hell.

"Behold I say unto you, that he that supposeth that little children need baptism is in the gall of bitterness and in the bonds of iniquity, for he hath neither faith, hope, nor charity; wherefore, should he be cut off while in the thought, he must go down to hell.

"For awful is the wickedness to suppose that God saveth one child because of baptism, and the other must perish because he hath no baptism.

"Wo be unto them that shall pervert the ways of the Lord after this manner, for they shall perish except they repent. Behold, I speak with boldness, having authority from God; and I fear not what man can do; for perfect love casteth out all fear.

"And I am filled with charity, which is everlasting love; wherefore, all children are alike unto me; wherefore I love little children with a perfect love; and they are all alike and partakers of salvation.

"For I know that God is not a partial God, neither a changeable being; but he is unchangeable from all eternity to all eternity.

"Little children cannot repent; wherefore, it is awful wickedness to deny the pure mercies of God unto them, for they are all alive in him because of his mercy.

"And he that saith that little children need baptism denieth the mercies of Christ, and setteth at naught the atonement of him and the power of his redemption.

"Wo unto such, for they are in danger of death, hell, and an endless torment. I speak it boldly; God hath commanded me. Listen unto them and give heed, or they stand against you at the judgment-seat of Christ.

"For behold that all little children are alive in Christ, and also all they that are without the law. For the power of redemption cometh on all them that have no law; wherefore, he that is not condemned, or he that is under no condemnation, cannot repent; and unto such baptism availeth nothing—

"But it is mockery before God, denying the mercies of Christ, and the power of his Holy Spirit, and putting trust in dead works.

"Behold, my son, this thing ought not to be; for repentance is unto them that are under condemnation and under the curse of a broken law.

"And the first fruits of repentance is baptism; and baptism cometh by faith unto the fulfilling the commandments; and the fulfilling the commandments bringeth remission of sins;

"And the remission of sins bringeth meekness and lowliness of heart; and because of meekness and lowliness of heart cometh the visitation of the Holy Ghost, which Comforter filleth with hope and perfect love, which love endureth by diligence unto prayer, until the end shall come, when all the saints shall dwell with God." (Moroni 8:8-26.)

The denominations of the world suppose that baptism is to remit the original sin of Adam, but of course this is in error.

The penalty for Adam's transgression was death, and baptism does not eliminate death. The word of the Lord to Adam was:

"But of the tree of the knowledge of good and evil, thou shalt not eat of it: for in the day that thou eatest thereof thou shalt surely die." (Genesis 2:17.)

The Apostle Paul confirmed this in his writings to the Romans:

"Wherefore, as by one man sin entered into the world, and death by sin; and so death passed upon all men, for that all have sinned." (Romans 5:12.)

He also explained the manner of atonement for that original sin in these words:

"But now is Christ risen from the dead, and become the firstfruits of them that slept.

"For since by man came death, by man came also the resurrection of the dead.

"For as in Adam all die, even so in Christ shall all be made alive." (1 Corinthians 15:20-22.)

The facts are simple and plain. Adam's sin brought physical death into the world. Christ's resurrection overcomes death; *baptism has nothing to do with it*. All will be resurrected—whether they are baptized or not, whether they believe in Christ or not. All mankind will be resurrected physically and literally from the grave.

Baptism is for the remission of our own personal sins, and not for Adam's transgression.

When we speak of baptism, we must also consider baptism for the dead.

Paul referred to it in his dissertation on the resurrection as recorded in the fifteenth chapter of 1 Corinthians. He was proving the fact of Christ's resurrection to the doubting Corinthians. One of his arguments was:

"Else what shall they do which are baptized for the dead, if the dead rise not at all? why are they then baptized for the dead?" (1 Corinthians 15:29.)

The Apostle Peter gave this explanation of the gospel being taken to the dead:

"For Christ also hath once suffered for sins, the just for the unjust, that he might bring us to God, being put to death in the flesh, but quickened by the Spirit:

"By which also he went and preached unto the spirits in prison;

"Which sometime were disobedient, when once the long-suffering of God waited in the days of Noah, while the ark was a preparing, wherein few, that is, eight souls were saved by water." (1 Peter 3:18-20.)

Then he added this important passage:

"For for this cause was the gospel preached also to them that are dead, that they might be judged according to men in the flesh, but live according to God in the spirit." (1 Peter 4:6.)

Dr. Hugh Nibley, of Brigham Young University, writing a series on the subject of baptism for the dead in the early Church, said this in the *Improvement Era*:

"In summing up the data at hand, we note three aspects of the documentary remains: their adequacy, their paucity, and their distribution. The three support and explain each other and lead to certain obvious conclusions.

"In the first place, the evidence is more than sufficient to establish the presence and prominence in the early church of belief in the salvation of the dead through ministrations that included preaching and baptism. The actual practice of vicarious baptism for the dead in the ancient church is equally certain, even the hostile commentators, with their seventeen different interpretations, agreeing on that one thing alone.

"Yet if they are clear and specific, references to baptism for the dead are nonetheless few. How is that to be explained in view of the extreme importance of the subject and the obvious popularity of the doctrine with the saints? For one thing the apostolic literature is not extensive; one volume could easily contain it all. Yet it is in these fragments of the earliest church writings that virtually all our references are to be found: the earlier a work is, the more it has to say about baptism for the dead. After the third century no one wants to touch the subject, all commentators confining themselves to repeating the same arguments against baptism for the dead and supplying the same farfetched and hair-splitting explanations of what Paul really meant. After the second century the vast barns of the *Patrologia* are virtually empty, and the fathers who love nothing so much as spinning out their long commentaries on every syllable of scripture pass by those passages of hope for the dead in peculiar silence. As Lanfranc put it, how can one presume to cope with a problem which has baffled the greatest minds of the church? It was the early church that preached and practised work for the dead, that no one denies; the later church, condemning the work, confesses at the same time that she does not understand it.

"As an example which we failed to include in the preceding article, a belated citation from the ninth century Bishop Aimon (Haymon) of Halberstadt, may be allowed at this point. Speaking of the primitive church he says: 'If one of their loved ones (friend or relative: *propinquus*) happened to depart this life without the grace of baptism, some living person would be baptized in his name: and they believed that the baptism of the living would profit the dead.' The Bishop must deny, of course, that Paul approved the practice, and has the usual difficulty explaining why the Apostle chose an improper practice to illustrate and support (*ut suadeat et ostendat*) his doctrine. (*Expositio* in *Ep. 1 Ad Cor.*, *PL cxvii*, 598.)" ("Baptism for the Dead in Ancient Times," *Improvement Era*, April 1949, page 214.)

Work for the dead was restored through the Prophet Joseph Smith following the coming of Elijah the Prophet. (See Malachi 4:5-6; D&C 110.) Baptisms for the dead were performed in Nauvoo, Illinois, before the Saints came west.

Again this was part of the restoration of all things, as Peter had said (see Acts 3:21), and it was also in preparation for the second coming of the Lord.

Fifteen

The Truth About Repentance

Temporary sorrow for sin is not acceptable to God. Neither is deathbed repentance. They do not meet the requirements of the law.

Repentance includes not only discontinuing the sin, but also making reconciliation with the aggrieved one and subsequently keeping the commandments for the rest of mortal life. Can we forget the Savior's words?

"Therefore if thou bring thy gift to the altar, and there rememberest that thy brother hath aught against thee;

"Leave there thy gift before the altar, and go thy way; first be reconciled to thy brother, and then come and offer thy gift." (Matthew 5:23-24.)

Repentance is not accomplished either by a mere confession or an admission of guilt. Repentance must include *lifetime reformation* in harmony with gospel teachings.

Said President David O. McKay:

"To repent—this we should note carefully—is to feel regret, contrition, or compunction for what one has done or omitted to do. It means to change one's mind in regard to past or intended actions or conduct on account of regret or dissatisfaction. It means to conquer selfishness, greed, jealousy, faultfinding, and slander. It means to control one's temper. It means to rise above the sordid things, which carnal nature would prompt us to do to gratify our appetites and passions, and to enter into the higher or spiritual realm.

"To repent is to change one's mind or one's heart with regard to past or intended action, conduct, etc., on account of regret or dissatisfaction." (*Gospel Ideals* [Salt Lake City: *Improvement Era*, 1953], page 14.)

On the same subject President Joseph F. Smith, one of our greatest doctrinal scholars, said:

"You cannot take a murderer, a suicide, an adulterer, a liar, or one who was or is thoroughly abominable in his life here, and simply by the performance of an ordinance of the gospel, cleanse him from sin and usher him into the presence of God. God has not instituted a plan of that kind, and it cannot be done. He has said you shall repent of your sins. The wicked will have to repent of their wickedness. Those who die without the knowledge of the gospel will have to come to the knowledge of it, and those who sin against light will have to pay the uttermost farthing for their transgression and their departure from the gospel, before they can ever get back to it. Do not forget that. Do not forget it, you elders in Israel, nor you mothers in Israel, either; and, when you seek to save either the living or the dead, bear it in mind that you can only do it on the principle of their repentance and acceptation of the plan of life. That is the only way in which you can succeed.

"I do not believe in the ideas that we hear sometimes advanced in the world, that it matters but little what men do in this life, if they will but confess Christ at the end of their journey in life, and that is all-sufficient, and that by so doing they will receive their passport into heaven. I denounce this doctrine. It is unscriptural, it is unreasonable, it is untrue, and it will not avail any man, no matter by whom this idea may be advocated; it will prove an utter failure unto men. As reasonable beings, as men and women of intelligence, we cannot help but admire and honor the doctrine of Jesus Christ, which is the doctrine of God, and which requires of every man and woman righteousness in their lives, purity in their thoughts, uprightness in their daily walk and conversation, devotion to the Lord, love of truth, love of their fellowman, and above all things in the world the love of God. These were the precepts that were inculcated by the Son of God when he walked among his brethren in the meridian of time. He taught these precepts; he exemplified them in his life, and advocated continually the doing of the will of him that sent him." (*Gospel Doctrine* [Salt Lake City: Deseret Book Company, 1939], page 95.)

President McKay then continued:

"The message of these young men who are going in all parts of the world, the message of the Church to all the world is: Repent of those things which contribute to the superiority of the physical senses over our love for spirituality. That is why they cry repentance! What does repentance mean? A *change* of life, a *change* of thought, a *change* of action. If you have been angry and hateful, change that hatred and enmity to love and consideration. If you have cheated a brother, let your conscience smite you and change that, and ask his forgiveness, and never do it again. In thus changing your life from those things which are on the animal plane, you repent of your sins. If you profane Deity, never do it again! Instead of profaning his name, worship him! And once that feeling of change comes to the soul, you desire to be born again, to have a new life.

"Then what is the next step in the gospel? Burying the old man with all that hatred and jealousy and sin.

"This changing of life, this repenting is what the world needs. It is a change of heart. Men must change their way of thinking! Change their way of feeling! Instead of hating and fighting and crushing one another, they should learn to love!

"Some men say you cannot change the lives of men, you cannot change their hearts.

"We proclaim that God has restored the gospel of Jesus Christ and made himself known again to man. We whisper to all the world, repent of the evils of your heart. Give your hearts to God instead of yourself, in selfishness. And then we proclaim, serve your fellow men instead of exploiting them. That is what

James had in mind when he said, ' . . . visit the fatherless and widows in their affliction. . . . ' (James 1:27.) Serve one another; make your livelihood, subdue nature, yes; cultivate your fields of beets, fields of potatoes, rye six feet tall, rectangular fields of wheat and of oats." (*Gospel Ideals*, page 328.)

Ezekiel was very specific about the doctrine of repentance. Said he:

"The soul that sinneth, it shall die. The son shall not bear the iniquity of the father, neither shall the father bear the iniquity of the son: the righteousness of the righteous shall be upon him, and the wickedness of the wicked shall be upon him.

"But if the wicked will turn from all his sins that he hath committed, and keep all my statutes, and do that which is lawful and right, he shall surely live, he shall not die.

"All his transgressions that he hath committed, they shall not be mentioned unto him: in his righteousness that he hath done he shall live.

"Have I any pleasure at all that the wicked should die? saith the Lord God: and not that he should return from his ways and live?

"But when the righteous turneth away from his righteousness, and committeth iniquity, and doeth according to all the abominations that the wicked man doeth, shall he live? All his righteousness that he hath done shall not be mentioned: in his trespass that he hath trespassed, and in his sin that he hath sinned, in them shall he die.

"Yet ye say, The way of the Lord is not equal. Hear now, O house of Israel; Is not my way equal? are not your ways unequal?

"When a righteous man turneth away from his righteousness, and committeth iniquity, and dieth in them; for his iniquity that he hath done shall he die.

"Again, when the wicked man turneth away from his wickedness that he hath committed, and doeth that which is lawful and right, he shall save his soul alive.

"Because he considereth, and turneth away from all his transgressions that he hath committed, he shall surely live, he shall not die.

"Yet saith the house of Israel, The way of the Lord is not equal. O house of Israel, are not my ways equal? are not your ways unequal?

"Therefore I will judge you, O house of Israel, every one according to his ways, saith the Lord God. Repent, and turn yourselves from all your transgressions; so iniquity shall not be your ruin.

"Cast away from you all your transgressions, whereby ye have transgressed; and make you a new heart and a new spirit: for why will ye die, O house of Israel?

"For I have no pleasure in the death of him that dieth, saith the Lord God: wherefore turn yourselves, and live ye." (Ezekiel 18:20-32.)

The Prophet Alma said this:

"And now, as I said unto you before, as ye have had so many witnesses, therefore, I beseech of you that ye do not procrastinate the day of your repentance until the end; for after this day of life, which is given us to prepare for eternity, behold, if we do not improve our time while in this life, then cometh the night of darkness wherein there can be no labor performed.

"Ye cannot say, when ye are brought to that awful crisis, that I will repent, that I will return to my God. Nay, ye cannot say this; for that same spirit which doth possess your bodies at the time that ye go out of this life, that same spirit will have power to possess your body in that eternal world.

"For behold, if ye have procrastinated the day of your repentance even until death, behold, ye have become subjected to the spirit of the devil, and he doth seal you his; therefore, the Spirit of the Lord hath withdrawn from you, and hath no place in you, and the devil hath all power over you; and this is the final state of the wicked.

"And this I know, because the Lord hath said he dwelleth not in unholy temples, but in the hearts of the righteous doth he dwell; yea, and he has also said that the righteous shall sit down in his kingdom, to go no more out; but their garments should be made white through the blood of the Lamb.

"And now, my beloved brethren, I desire that ye should remember these things, and that ye should work out your salvation with fear before God, and that ye should no more deny the coming of Christ." (Alma 34:33-37.)

The Prophet Abinadi had this sober advice:

"But remember that he that persists in his own carnal nature, and goes on in the ways of sin and rebellion against God, remaineth in his fallen state and the devil hath all power over him. Therefore, he is as though there was no redemption made, being an enemy to God; and also is the devil an enemy to God." (Mosiah 16:5.)

The Lord has made it clear that no unclean thing may enter his presence; and if we hope to do so, we must cleanse ourselves of all our wickedness, repent fully, and live the gospel for the remaining part of our lives.

But repentance is insufficient without baptism in water for the remission of sins.

Merely discontinuing the sin (or confessing it and saying we are sorry) does not cleanse us of the guilt. After we have done all we can to make reconciliation, to readjust our lives, and to keep the laws of God, baptism still awaits us; for that is the ordinance by which we receive the cleansing.

Can we forget the words of Peter as he addressed the multitude?

"Now when they heard this, they were pricked in their heart, and said unto Peter and to the rest of the apostles, Men and brethren, what shall we do?

"Then Peter said unto them, Repent, and be baptized every one of you in the name of Jesus Christ for the remission of sins, and ye shall receive the gift of the Holy Ghost." (Acts 2:37-38.)

John the Baptist taught that the ordinance was for the remission of sins. (See Mark 1:4; Luke 3:3.)

When Paul was converted, what did Ananias say to him?

"And now why tarriest thou? arise, and be baptized, and wash away thy sins, calling on the name of the Lord." (Acts 22:16.)

And so it is with us.

The most emphatic direction we have on the subject of repentance comes from the Lord himself:

"Therefore I command you to repent—repent, lest I smite

you by the rod of my mouth, and by my wrath, and by my anger, and your sufferings be sore—how sore you know not, how exquisite you know not, yea, how hard to bear you know not.

"For behold, I, God, have suffered these things for all, that they might not suffer if they would repent;

"But if they would not repent they must suffer even as I;

"Which suffering caused myself, even God, the greatest of all, to tremble because of pain and to bleed at every pore, and to suffer both body and spirit—and would that I might not drink the bitter cup and shrink—

"Nevertheless, glory be to the Father, and I partook and finished my preparations unto the children of men." (D&C 19:15-19.)

The easy repentance of the world has no place in the kingdom of God.

When the angels announced the coming of John the Baptist, they made it clear that John would prepare a people for the Lord. (See Luke 1:76-77.)

The same thing is true of the Prophet Joseph Smith. Those who respond to his teachings must believe the gospel, repent, and be washed free of their sins. How else could a people be prepared for the coming of the Lord?

This the Prophet Joseph did; and the work is now being and will continue to be carried on. The way is being prepared for the Lord.

Sixteen

The Destiny of Man

Could a people prepare for the coming of the Lord if they did not understand their relationship with him? Could they prepare goals and plans to make their mortal life harmonize with the next life if they were not told of their ultimate destiny? What is the final destiny of man?

There are those who still believe in annihilation—that everything ends with death. Even scientific men are now rejecting this theory, feeling that man's intelligence and his possibilities for advancement cannot be wasted forever in death.

Then there are those who believe that the spirit sleeps in the grave until resurrection day, when only the spirit will come forth—not the body—to some kind of unexplainable eternal existence of joy and bliss.

And then there are some people who think that the righteous will spend eternity gazing at the celestial face of God in a beatific vision. It is also believed that some may sing and play harps. Could intelligent people be forever satisfied with that? Marvelous as it will be to behold the face of the Almighty, not even he would be satisfied to have his children do that as an everlasting, unchanging occupation.

He wants his children to progress, to grow, to develop, as parents do for their children here on earth. And such progression requires study, work, and a good deal of planning.

The difficulty is that since the light of the gospel was extinguished by the apostasy, mankind lost with it the true concept and understanding of God. Without that, no one could know of man's destiny.

To know the ultimate place of man in eternity, we must understand that since we are the offspring of God, we actually can become like him. That is our destiny. (See Acts 17:28-29; Hebrews 12:9; Romans 8:16-17; D&C 84:37-41.)

It was no idle command that the Savior gave us when he said: "Be ye therefore perfect, even as your Father which is in heaven is perfect." (Matthew 5:48.)

It is normal in this life for children to become like their parents, and it is equally normal and natural for us to become like our Father in Heaven, since we are his literal spirit offspring. We have divinity within us. We are to be his heirs—even joint heirs with Jesus Christ.

The full significance of those words is still beyond our finite minds, but we do have some understanding of them. The Lord said to the Prophet Joseph Smith:

"And he that receiveth me receiveth my Father;

"And he that receiveth my Father receiveth my Father's kingdom; therefore all that my Father hath shall be given unto him." (D&C 84:37-38.)

"All that my Father hath shall be given unto him"! The words are staggering yet true, and they may be fulfilled in our eternal existence if we are worthy of such a reward.

The true concept of the Fatherhood of God (which includes our becoming like him) and the proper understanding of the brotherhood of man (we are all God's children) came with the restoration of the gospel through the Prophet Joseph Smith.

The description of the three degrees of glory as provided in the Doctrine and Covenants, section 76, is most enlightening and should be read and studied by all. It is one of the most important revelations the Lord has given.

President Joseph Fielding Smith, one of our most astute

gospel authorities, discoursed on this subject at length and in a most understandable way. Said he:

"The exaltation to the celestial kingdom is so great that the Father is fully justified in making it dependent upon strict obedience to *all* of his commandments. The celestial kingdom is a kingdom of perfection. All who enter there must be thoroughly tried and proved and become perfect to inherit it. The Lord has said that through their obedience those who enter must be sanctified from all unrighteousness. Every law governing it must be obeyed. There can be no opposition to divine law, nor could any one receiving this reward have any desire to change or disagree with anything prevailing there, for these laws are perfect. As well may a man in the mortal world object to the law of gravity or any of the other fixed laws of nature, as to object to the laws of the celestial kingdom. They have been tried, proved and are eternal. This being the fact there can be nothing but peace and joy in that kingdom.

"Exalted beings, because they have proved themselves by obedience to 'every word that proceedeth forth from the mouth of God,' will become perfect and be like him, and as heirs will become gods themselves. The history of mankind has revealed most clearly, that from the beginning men have been rebellious, with few exceptions, disobeying the laws of God that would bring them to perfection. The words of the Savior in the Sermon on the Mount are full of meaning; but they have been ignored and in many instances misunderstood. As an example, when he said to those who were present on the memorable occasion, 'Be ye therefore perfect, even as your Father which is in heaven is perfect,' some argue that he did not mean just what he said. It has been maintained by some members of the Church that he meant this relatively, for we cannot be perfect as God is perfect. The fact is, however, that he intended it to mean just what he said—for those who believe on him to seek the same kind of perfection which his Father has. He was not speaking as pertaining to mortality, but with the larger view embracing eternity itself. We well understand that mortal man cannot be perfect, but the immortal man can. To reach that condition will take time and we have eternity for it, for we are destined to live forever. In the revelations given to the Church in this last dispensation this matter of perfection, yet to come, is made very clear. One of the most profound thoughts ever given by revelation is this given to the Prophet Joseph Smith:

" 'And that which doth not edify is not of God, and is darkness.

" 'That which is of God is light; and he that receiveth light, and continueth in God, receiveth more light; and that light groweth brighter and brighter until the perfect day.'

"It is here made perfectly plain that it is possible for man, *if he will continue in God*, to obtain eventually the fulness of light and this light is knowledge and wisdom. But this will not come in the few years allotted to man in mortality. Again the Lord said:

" 'And this greater priesthood [i.e. Melchizedek Priesthood] administereth the gospel and holdeth the keys of the mysteries of the kingdom, even the keys of the knowledge of God.

" 'Therefore, in the ordinances thereof, the power of godliness is manifest.

" 'And without the ordinances thereof, and the authority of the priesthood, the power of godliness is not manifest unto men in the flesh;

" 'For without this no man can see the face of God, even the Father, and live.'

"Once again the Lord said:

" 'The Spirit of truth is of God. I am the Spirit of truth, and John bore record of me, saying: He receiveth a fulness of truth, yea, even of all truth;

" 'And no man receiveth a fulness unless he keepeth his commandments.

" 'He that keepeth his commandments receiveth truth and light, until he is glorified in truth and knoweth all things.'

"In these scriptures the Lord most emphatically declared that it is impossible for man to become like God without the Priesthood and obedience to his commandments. Man has the power to know all things, to become perfect and be bathed in light, knowledge and wisdom, if he will only humble himself and walk in the light and truth. The man who refuses and lives bound within his own wisdom can never attain to these great blessings of exaltation and progression. A man must have, and be obedient to, the power of the Priesthood; he must be in full harmony and fellowship with God from whom all knowledge, wisdom and power come. No matter how much knowledge a man may gain, in this life or in the life to come, he cannot obtain the fulness unless he holds and magnifies the Priesthood and *continueth in God!* The power, knowledge and wisdom in their fulness, will never be exercised by those who reject the counsels and covenants of the Gospel of Jesus Christ. These are the possessions to be given to the just and true, who become members of the Church of the Firstborn.

"All men who become heirs of God and joint heirs with Jesus Christ will have to receive the fulness of the ordinances of his kingdom; and those who will not receive all the ordinances will come short of the fulness of that glory, if they do not lose the whole.

"When this celestialized earth comes, then only those of the celestial kingdom will inherit it. Those who have lived a terrestrial law will be assigned to a terrestrial kingdom on some other globe. Those who have lived a telestial law will have to go to a telestial sphere suited to their condition. Where these worlds are the Lord has not revealed to us, however they are spheres now being prepared for them. Justice demands that every man shall receive a reward according to his works. Those who do not attain to eternal life, which is to become sons and daughters of God and joint heirs with Jesus Christ, will receive the gift of immortality. Immortality means that they will live forever. The bodies of all the children of men, both the righteous and the unrighteous, even sons of perdition, will come forth in the resurrection, their spirits and bodies being united inseparably, and they shall live forever. Eternal life has a deeper meaning than immortality, and all those who receive it become like God. They will inherit the fulness of the Father's kingdom, all things will be given to them and they become sons and daughters of God. In the celestial kingdom those who receive the exaltation will remain husbands and wives. The family organization will not be broken and will endure forever and they will have eternal increase.

"In the terrestrial and telestial kingdoms, there will be no marriage, hence no continuation of the lives, for they remain in these kingdoms separately and singly through all eternity. This the Lord calls 'the deaths,' because there is no increase. The question frequently arises: 'If men and women live singly in the terrestrial and the telestial kingdoms, then what will prevent them from living promiscuously?' The Lord has given us the answer to that question. They will be quickened by different kind of bodies. They shall receive back their natural body, but they will be terrestrial bodies and telestial bodies and their bodies will be suited to the conditions prevailing in those kingdoms. Elder Orson Pratt has given an excellent explanation as follows:

" 'In every species of animals and plants there are many resemblances in the general outline, and many specific differences characterizing the individuals of each species. So in the resurrection: There will be several classes of resurrected bodies; some celestial, some terrestrial, some telestial, and some sons of perdition. Each of these classes will differ from the others by prominent and marked distinctions; yet in each, considered by itself, there will be found many resemblances as well as distinctions. There will be some physical peculiarity by which each individual in every class can be identified.'

"Those who inherit the terrestrial kingdom and the telestial kingdom do not go into the presence of God our Eternal Father. Those who inherit the telestial kingdom will be ministered to by those of the terrestrial, and those of the terrestrial by those of the celestial. The inhabitants of the terrestrial will have visitations from Jesus Christ, but not the Father. This kingdom will be inhabited by those who have lived good moral lives, who have been honest, honorable and just, but who would not receive the Gospel with its covenants. The telestial kingdom will be the place for the wicked, those 'who are liars, and sorcerers, and adulterers, and whoremongers, and whosoever loves and makes a lie. These are they who suffer the wrath of God on the earth. These are they who suffer the vengeance of eternal fire.

These are they who are cast down to hell and suffer the wrath of Almighty God, until the fulness of times, when Christ shall have subdued all enemies under his feet, and shall have perfected his work; When he shall deliver up the kingdom, and present it unto the Father, spotless, saying; I have overcome and have trodden the wine-press alone, even the wine-press of the fierceness of the wrath of Almighty God.'

"There is still another group, comparatively few, who, after receiving the fulness of the Gospel and the testimony of Jesus, then deny him and put him to open shame by turning against his work and denying his power. These are called sons of perdition and they go away into outer darkness.

"So the Lord in his great mercy does for all men just the best that he can. Even the wicked, after they pay the price, and they will have to pay a dreadful price, will be placed in a kingdom where they can be made as happy as circumstances will permit. Through their intense suffering while they wait for the resurrection at the end of the earth's temporal existence, they will have learned to be obedient to law, for this will be a requirement in each of the kingdoms, but where God and Christ are they cannot come worlds without end." (*Man: His Origin and Destiny* [Salt Lake City: Deseret Book Company, 1965], pages 532-541.)

Seventeen

To All the World

When the Savior described his second coming to the ancient apostles, he pointed out that one of the important things to be done in the latter days in preparation for his coming would be that the gospel would be preached in all the world as a witness to all peoples—and *then* the end would come.

As this is given in the inspired translation, found in the Pearl of Great Price, we read:

"For as the light of the morning cometh out of the east, and shineth even unto the west, and covereth the whole earth, so shall also the coming of the Son of Man be.

"And now I show unto you a parable. Behold, wheresoever the carcass is, there will the eagles be gathered together; so likewise shall mine elect be gathered from the four quarters of the earth.

"And they shall hear of wars and rumors of wars.

"Behold I speak for mine elect's sake; for nation shall rise against nation, and kingdom against kingdom; there shall be famines, and pestilences, and earthquakes, in divers places.

"And again, because iniquity shall abound, the love of many shall wax cold; but he that shall not be overcome, the same shall be saved.

"And again, this Gospel of the Kingdom shall be preached in all the world, for a witness unto all nations, and then shall the end come, or the destruction of the wicked." (Joseph Smith 1:26-31.)

But as we have already discussed, the gospel was taken from the earth through the great falling away. But Peter said that it would be restored. (See Acts 3:21.)

John in his revelation explained that the gospel would come back to earth by means of an angel flying through the midst of heaven in the hour of God's judgment. (See Revelation 14:6-7.)

In making this prediction John also declared that the gospel was to be taken to all nations "in the hour of God's judgment."

It would be the same "going forth" of the gospel as referred to by the Savior; for there is only one gospel, and the predictions are parallel.

The gospel was restored, as we have shown. It is now (1979) being taken to all the free world by an army of more than twenty-seven thousand missionaries who are laboring in sixty different nations and teaching in more than a score of different languages.

Through the missionary effort converts are coming into the Church by the hundreds of thousands.

The Church membership is doubling every ten to twelve years. We have an increasing number of missions. We have more than a thousand stakes with well above four million members, located in most of the free nations. We have more than a quarter of a million members of the Church in South America, and over two hundred thousand in Mexico and Central America, with many stakes in both areas.

In Great Britain where we have one hundred thousand members, we have eight missions and thirty stakes. We have stakes and missions in France, Belgium, the Germanic countries, all the Scandinavian countries, in South Africa, Alaska, the Orient, and down through the islands of the sea to Australia.

In fulfilment of the prophecies, the gospel indeed is going to all the world as the Savior predicted and as John saw in his revelation.

When we are allowed by governments to enter countries where now there is no religious freedom, it will be a happy day and missionaries will be provided.

The prophecies are being fulfilled. The preparation is going forward for the coming of the Savior.

The Lord has said this would be a time of tribulation. He explained:

"And again shall the abomination of desolation, spoken of by Daniel the prophet, be fulfilled.

"And immediately after the tribulation of those days, the sun shall be darkened, and the moon shall not give her light, and the stars shall fall from heaven, and the powers of heaven shall be shaken.

"Verily, I say unto you, this generation, in which these things shall be shown forth, shall not pass away until all I have told you shall be fulfilled.

"Although, the days will come, that heaven and earth shall pass away; yet my words shall not pass away, but all shall be fulfilled.

"And, as I said before, after the tribulation of those days, and the powers of the heavens shall be shaken, then shall appear the sign of the Son of Man in heaven, and then shall all the tribes of the earth mourn; and they shall see the Son of Man coming in the clouds of heaven, with power and great glory;

"And whoso treasureth up my word, shall not be deceived, for the Son of Man shall come, and he shall send his angels before him with the great sound of a trumpet, and they shall gather together the remainder of his elect from the four winds, from one end of heaven to the other.

"Now learn a parable of the fig-tree—When its branches are yet tender, and it begins to put forth leaves, you know that summer is nigh at hand;

"So likewise, mine elect, when they shall see all these things, they shall know that he is near, even at the doors;

"But of that day, and hour, no one knoweth; no, not the angels of God in heaven, but my Father only.

"But as it was in the days of Noah, so it shall be also at the coming of the Son of Man;

"For it shall be with them, as it was in the days which were before the flood; for until the day that Noah entered into the ark they were eating and drinking, marrying and giving in marriage;

"And knew not until the flood came, and took them all away; so shall also the coming of the Son of Man be.

"Then shall be fulfilled that which is written, that in the last days, two shall be in the field, and one shall be taken, and the other left;

"Two shall be grinding at the mill, the one shall be taken, and the other left;

"And what I say unto one, I say unto all men; watch, therefore, for you know not at what hour your Lord doth come.

"But know this, if the good man of the house had known in what watch the thief would come, he would have watched, and would not have suffered his house to have been broken up, but would have been ready.

"Therefore be ye also ready, for in such an hour as ye think not, the Son of Man cometh.

"Who, then, is a faithful and wise servant, whom his lord hath made ruler over his household, to give them meat in due season?

"Blessed is that servant whom his lord, when he cometh, shall find so doing; and verily I say unto you, he shall make him ruler over all his goods.

"But if that evil servant shall say in his heart: My lord delayeth his coming,

"And shall begin to smite his fellow-servants, and to eat and drink with the drunken.

"The lord of that servant shall come in a day when he looketh not for him, and in an hour that he is not aware of,

"And shall cut him asunder, and shall appoint him his portion with the hypocrites; there shall be weeping and gnashing of teeth.

"And thus cometh the end of the wicked, according to the prophecy of Moses, saying: They shall be cut off from among the people; but the end of the earth is not yet, but by and by." (Joseph Smith 1:32-55.)

All of the preparation for the second coming of the Lord arises out of the restoration of the gospel through the Prophet Joseph Smith, the great forerunner for the Christ in the last days.

Eighteen

Temples of the Lord

When Malachi spoke of the coming of the Lord he said: "And the Lord, whom ye seek, shall suddenly come to his temple." (Malachi 3:1.)

What temple is referred to?

It could not possibly be the temple at Jerusalem because that was destroyed in A.D. 70 so that not one stone stood upon the other. (Matthew 24:2.)

In the passage by Malachi, reference to the Savior's coming to the temple included the announcement that he would send his messenger to prepare the way *and then* he would suddenly come to his temple.

That indicates that the messenger sent to prepare the way before the Lord would be a temple builder.

Obviously the Lord would not come to some worldly temple or mosque or synagogue or even to the Taj Mahal. Why? Because his messenger sent to prepare the way did not build any of them, and they are not according to God's design.

The messenger was to be a temple builder. The temple would not be of man's design nor one of worldly use. It would be a temple of the Most High God. It will only be to this, *his own temple*, that the Lord will come. He would have no reason to appear in a temple where man's form of worship is conducted. Worship by man's creeds is in vain. (See Matthew 15:9.)

What else do the scriptures say about this matter?

Both Isaiah and Micah refer to this subject. Isaiah said:

"And it shall come to pass in the last days, that the mountain of the Lord's house shall be established in the top of the mountains, and shall be exalted above the hills; and all nations shall flow unto it.

"And many people shall go and say, Come ye, and let us go up to the mountain of the Lord, to the house of the God of Jacob; and he will teach us of his ways, and we will walk in his paths: for out of Zion shall go forth the law, and the word of the Lord from Jerusalem.

"And he shall judge among the nations, and shall rebuke many people: and they shall beat their swords into plowshares, and their spears into pruninghooks: nation shall not lift up sword against nation, neither shall they learn war any more." (Isaiah 2:2-4.)

Micah wrote the prophecy in this manner:

"But in the last days it shall come to pass, that the mountain of the house of the Lord shall be established in the top of the mountains, and it shall be exalted above the hills; and people shall flow unto it.

"And many nations shall come, and say, Come, and let us go up to the mountain of the Lord, and to the house of the God of Jacob; and he will teach us of his ways, and we will walk in his paths: for the law shall go forth of Zion, and the word of the Lord from Jerusalem.

"And he shall judge among many people, and rebuke strong nations afar off; and they shall beat their swords into plowshares, and their spears into pruninghooks; nation shall not lift up a sword against nation, neither shall they learn war any more.

"But they shall sit every man under his vine and under his fig tree; and none shall make them afraid: for the mouth of the Lord of hosts hath spoken it.

"For all people will walk every one in the name of his god, and we will walk in the name of the Lord our God for ever and ever.

"In that day, saith the Lord, will I assemble her that halteth, and I will gather her that is driven out, and her that I have afflicted;

"And I will make her that halted a remnant, and her that was cast far off a strong nation: and the Lord shall reign over them in mount Zion from henceforth, even for ever." (Micah 4:1-7.)

Only among the Latter-day Saints can these prophecies find fulfillment. They are the temple builders, and Joseph began the work in his day. It has been carried on ever since in a glorious manner.

Modern temple building began in Kirtland, Ohio, under the command of the Lord. The first temple of the Church, built in that city, still stands and is a center of interest to visitors who go there.

Attempts were made by the members of the Church, under the leadership of the Prophet Joseph, to build temples at Far West, and Independence, Missouri, but persecution prevented it. When there was a lull in persecution, however, the Latter-day Saints erected a beautiful structure at Nauvoo, Illinois. It was begun under the direction of the Prophet Joseph, but he was martyred before it was completed. Under the leadership of President Brigham Young it was completed, and hundreds of ordinances were performed within its sacred walls.

But Isaiah and Micah both declared that the house of the Lord spoken of in their prophecies would be built in the tops of the mountains, in a place exalted above the hills.

It is interesting that the Roman Catholic Bible, known as the Knox Translation, gives Micah's announcement in this language:

"The Temple Hill! One day it shall stand there, highest of all the mountain-heights, overtopping the peaks of them, and the nations will flock there together. A multitude of people will make their way to it, crying, Come let us climb up to the Lord's mountain peak, to the house where the God of Jacob dwells; he shall teach us the right way, we will walk in the paths he has chosen."

The Latter-day Saint pioneers of 1847 had been in the Salt Lake Valley, in "the tops of the mountains," only four days when President Brigham Young designated the place for the erection of the temple.

The construction required forty years. It was done in the poverty of the people; but this temple is regarded as one of the most beautiful and unusual buildings in the world.

It is the temple of the Lord. It is high in the mountains, well above the hills, and many people are coming to it.

Every year more than two million tourists come to view it. They represent nearly all the nations of the free world and sometimes nations from behind the iron curtain.

They come and many seek the truth. They are guided through the visitors' centers on that block and are taught the gospel.

The prophecies of Isaiah and Micah therefore are in the process of fulfilment, which began when the Salt Lake Temple was erected on a location nearly a mile above sea level.

Now the Church is continuing the work and building other temples in various parts of the world. They are dedicated houses of the Lord, all in preparation for the coming of the Lord.

Why are temples so important? Because within them ordinances are provided which cannot be given anywhere else. They are saving ordinances in the same sense in which baptism is.

Realizing the need to have these blessings for their eventual exaltation in the kingdom of heaven, the Saints have made tremendous sacrifices in both time and money for the construction of temples. And God has rewarded them for it.

Nineteen

Members Called Saints

One other thing that was restored, but is seldom mentioned in this connection, is the name by which the members of Christ's true Church are known—Saints.

This seems like a little thing, but is nevertheless significant. It is one of the marks of identification of the true Church.

Webster's dictionary says that any believer in the early Christian Church was known as a Saint. The Bible dictionaries agree.

The members of the early Church were not known as Christians until the name was thrust on them in pagan Antioch (see Acts 11:26) about A.D. 43. It was a nickname and was given in derision when they were persecuted. The name of Christ was hated. The "Christian Church" was everywhere spoken against. (See Acts 28:22.)

But in the sacred brotherhood of the Church the members were called Saints, as Paul's epistles make abundantly clear. For example we have:

"To all that be in Rome, beloved of God, called to be saints: Grace to you and peace from God our Father, and the Lord Jesus Christ." (Romans 1:7.)

"Unto the church of God which is at Corinth, to them that are sanctified in Christ Jesus, called to be saints, with all that in every place call upon the name of Jesus Christ our Lord, both theirs and ours." (1 Corinthians 1:2.)

"Paul, an apostle of Jesus Christ by the will of God, and Timothy our brother, unto the church of God which is at Corinth, with all the saints which are in all Achaia." (2 Corinthians 1:1.)

"Paul, an apostle of Jesus Christ by the will of God, to the saints which are at Ephesus, and to the faithful in Christ Jesus." (Ephesians 1:1.)

"Paul and Timotheus, the servants of Jesus Christ, to all the saints in Christ Jesus which are at Philippi, with the bishops and deacons." (Philippians 1:1.)

"To the saints and faithful brethren in Christ which are at Colosse: Grace be unto you, and peace, from God our Father and the Lord Jesus Christ." (Colossians 1:2.)

The custom of venerating dead Christians of prominence and conferring upon them the title of Saint was a later innovation.

When the Lord directed the organization of his modern Church through the Prophet Joseph Smith, He instructed that it should be called The Church of Jesus Christ of Latter-day Saints. The "latter-day" designation was given to distinguish it from the Church as organized anciently.

"And also unto my faithful servants who are of the high council of my church in Zion, for thus it shall be called, and unto all the elders and people of my Church of Jesus Christ of Latter-day Saints, scattered abroad in all the world;

"For thus shall my church be called in the last days, even The Church of Jesus Christ of Latter-day Saints." (D&C 115:3-4.)

To live a "saintly life" then simply means to live the kind of life a Latter-day Saint should live. And what is that? It is to keep the commandments of the gospel.

The Saints are a covenant people. And what are the covenants for? To help us keep the commandments.

The Savior taught that if we love him we must keep his commandments. He said:

"I am the vine, ye are the branches: He that abideth in me,

and I in him, the same bringeth forth much fruit: for without me ye can do nothing.

"If a man abide not in me, he is cast forth as a branch, and is withered; and men gather them, and cast them into the fire, and they are burned.

"If ye abide in me, and my words abide in you, ye shall ask what ye will, and it shall be done unto you.

"Herein is my Father glorified, that ye bear much fruit; so shall ye be my disciples.

"As the Father hath loved me, so have I loved you: continue ye in my love.

"If ye keep my commandments, ye shall abide in my love; even as I have kept my Father's commandments, and abide in his love.

"These things have I spoken unto you, that my joy might remain in you, and that your joy might be full.

"This is my commandment, That ye love one another, as I have loved you.

"Greater love hath no man than this, that a man lay down his life for his friends.

"Ye are my friends, if ye do whatsoever I command you.

"Henceforth I call you not servants; for the servant knoweth not what his lord doeth: but I have called you friends; for all things that I have heard of my Father I have made known unto you." (John 15:5-15.)

The Lord said this in modern times:

"And I now give unto you a commandment to beware concerning yourselves, to give diligent heed to the words of eternal life.

"For you shall live by every word that proceedeth forth from the mouth of God.

"For the word of the Lord is truth, and whatsoever is truth is light, and whatsoever is light is Spirit, even the Spirit of Jesus Christ.

"And the Spirit giveth light to every man that cometh into the world; and the Spirit enlighteneth every man through the world, that hearkeneth to the voice of the Spirit.

"And every one that hearkeneth to the voice of the Spirit cometh unto God, even the Father.

"And the Father teacheth him of the covenant which he has renewed and confirmed upon you, which is confirmed upon you for your sakes, and not for your sakes only, but for the sake of the whole world.

"And the whole world lieth in sin, and groaneth under darkness and under the bondage of sin.

"And by this you may know they are under the bondage of sin, because they come not unto me.

"For whoso cometh not unto me is under the bondage of sin.

"And whoso receiveth not my voice is not acquainted with my voice, and is not of me.

"And by this you may know the righteous from the wicked, and that the whole world groaneth under sin and darkness even now." (D&C 84:43-53.)

The presidents of the Church have made constant appeals to parents to so conduct themselves that they will be examples of "saintly living" and to do all they can to keep our communities clean so that young people may grow up in a proper environment.

President David O. McKay commented on this as follows:

"That there is a threatening increase in delinquency in our communities, particularly among boys and girls of high school age, is all too apparent to anyone who will open his eyes to see and his ears to hear; and steps should be taken to curtail this delinquency.

"It is with this purpose in mind that I refer not to the delinquency of youth but to the delinquency of adults.

"Youth is influenced by example and environment. Dominating groups exerting this influence are the home, the church, the school, social circles, and civic conditions.

"There are too many delinquent fathers and mothers. Our homes are the centers that determine the type of our citizenry. To dignify home and parenthood is one of the noblest aims of human society. The greatest responsibility given to woman is the divine gift to be a mother. She thus blessed, who has health and opportunity, and shirks the responsibility for social prestige and pleasure, is recreant to her duty as wife and mother. The father, particularly, if he be a member of the Church and holds the priesthood, who fails to set a proper example before his children is a delinquent and is a contributor to child delinquency.

"Upon the responsibility of parents to have proper home environment, modern revelation is most explicit:

" 'And again, inasmuch as parents have children in Zion, or in any of her stakes which are organized, that teach them not to understand the doctrine of repentance, faith in Christ the Son of the living God, and of baptism and the gift of the Holy Ghost by the laying on of the hands, when eight years old, the sin be upon the heads of the parents.

" 'For this shall be a law unto the inhabitants of Zion, or in any of her stakes which are organized.

" 'And their children shall be baptized for the remission of their sins when eight years old, and receive the laying on of the hands.

" 'And they shall also teach their children to pray, and to walk uprightly before the Lord.' (D&C 68:25-28.)

"Quarreling among parents and children, faultfinding, backbiting, smoking cigarettes, drinking intoxicating liquors, using profane language, make a home environment that contributes to delinquency. No parent can consistently teach faith in Christ who profanes the name of Deity. Profanity is never heard in the well-ordered home. Swearing is a vice that bespeaks a low standard of breeding. Blasphemous exclamations drive out all spirit of reverence. Irreverence is always a mark of delinquency." (*Gospel Ideals,* pages 419-420.)

Twenty

Eight Things

The scriptures set forth that eight things shall take place in the latter days to prepare the way of the Lord. They are:

1.   The Lord will set up his kingdom which shall never be destroyed nor given to another people, in fulfillment of the prediction of Daniel the Prophet. (See Daniel 2:44.)

2.   The house of the Lord will be erected in the tops of the mountains. (See Micah 4:1; Isaiah 2:2.)

3.   There will be a restoration before or incident to the Second Coming of all things whatsoever God has spoken by the mouth of all his holy prophets from the beginning of the world. (See Acts 3:21.)

4.   An angel will fly through the midst of heaven in the hour of God's judgment, bringing the gospel back to earth.

5.   The gospel will be preached to all the world as a witness to all nations, and then the end will come. (See Matthew 24:14; Revelation 14:6-7.)

6.   A new volume of scripture will be brought forth "out of the ground" and through it an ancient nation, destroyed

suddenly, will speak "low out of the dust." The "stick of Ephraim" (the Book of Mormon) will be made a companion volume to the "stick of Judah" (the Bible) in the latter days. (See Isaiah 29; Ezekiel 37:15-28.)

7.   The Prophet Elijah will come back before the great and dreadful day of the Lord to turn the hearts of fathers and children toward each other. (See Malachi 4:5.)

8.   Israel will be gathered before the Lord comes.

Most of these events have already transpired. The preparation for the Second Coming is being accomplished.

The gospel has been restored; the Church of Jesus Christ is again organized on the earth. And as Daniel said, it will never be destroyed or given to another people.

Temples have been built in the tops of the mountains and even overseas.

The gospel is being preached in all the free nations.

The new volume of scripture has been produced and published. It is the Book of Mormon.

The Prophet Elijah came to earth April 3, 1836, appearing in the Kirtland Temple and conferring on Joseph Smith and Oliver Cowdery the powers pertaining to temple work.

Moses came to Joseph on the same day and conferred on him the keys of the gathering of Israel.

There was no concerted movement on the part of the Jews to return to Palestine until after that land was freed from the Turks in the First World War. The British army led by General Allenby marched into Jerusalem in 1917. Under the Balfour agreement Britain and the United States sponsored settlement of the Jews "in their homeland."

Now some three million Jews are living in Palestine. They have established their own nation of Israel and have fought repeated wars for their very existence. The Lord has promised that they will remain there. It will be to Palestine the Lord will come to make an appearance to the Jews in the period of Armageddon. The Jews at that time will be besieged by armies from the north seeking their destruction. Much of the city of Jerusalem will be destroyed. The Jews will flee from their besieged city to the Mount of Olives. There the Lord will appear to them, and show them the marks of the Crucifixion, when they will finally accept him as their Messiah. (See Zechariah 12, 13, 14; Ezekiel 38; D&C 45.) Concerning this the Lord has said:

"Hearken, O ye people of my church, saith the Lord your God, and hear the word of the Lord concerning you—

"The Lord who shall suddenly come to his temple; the Lord who shall come down upon the world with a curse to judgment; yea, upon all the nations that forget God, and upon all the ungodly among you.

"For he shall make bare his holy arm in the eyes of all the nations, and all the ends of the earth shall see the salvation of their God.

"Wherefore, prepare ye, prepare ye, O my people; sanctify yourselves; gather ye together, O ye people of my church, upon the land of Zion, all you that have not been commanded to tarry.

"Go ye out from Babylon. Be ye clean that bear the vessels of the Lord.

"Call your solemn assemblies, and speak often one to another. And let every man call upon the name of the Lord.

"Yea, verily I say unto you again, the time has come when the voice of the Lord is unto you: Go ye out of Babylon; gather ye out from among the nations, from the four winds, from one end of heaven to the other.

"Send forth the elders of my church unto the nations which are afar off; unto the islands of the sea; send forth unto foreign lands; call upon all nations, first upon the Gentiles, and then upon the Jews.

"And behold, and lo, this shall be their cry, and the voice of the Lord unto all people: Go ye forth unto the land of Zion, that the borders of my people may be enlarged, and that her stakes may be strengthened, and that Zion may go forth unto the regions round about.

"Yea, let the cry go forth among all people: Awake and arise and go forth to meet the Bridegroom; behold and lo, the Bridegroom cometh; go ye out to meet him. Prepare yourselves for the great day of the Lord.

"Watch, therefore, for ye know neither the day nor the hour.

"Let them, therefore, who are among the Gentiles flee unto Zion.

"And let them who be of Judah flee unto Jerusalem, unto the mountains of the Lord's house.

"Go ye out from among the nations, even from Babylon, from the midst of wickedness, which is spiritual Babylon.

"But verily, thus saith the Lord, let not your flight be in haste, but let all things be prepared before you; and he that goeth, let him not look back lest sudden destruction shall come upon him.

"Hearken and hear, O ye inhabitants of the earth. Listen, ye elders of my church together, and hear the voice of the Lord; for he calleth upon all men, and he commandeth all men everywhere to repent.

"For behold, the Lord God hath sent forth the angel crying through the midst of heaven, saying: Prepare ye the way of the Lord, and make his paths straight, for the hour of his coming is nigh—

"When the Lamb shall stand upon Mount Zion, and with him a hundred and forty-four thousand, having his Father's name written on their foreheads.

"Wherefore, prepare ye for the coming of the Bridegroom; go ye, go ye out to meet him.

"For behold, he shall stand upon the mount of Olivet, and upon the mighty ocean, even the great deep, and upon the islands of the sea, and upon the land of Zion.

"And he shall utter his voice out of Zion, and he shall speak from Jerusalem, and his voice shall be heard among all people;

"And it shall be a voice as the voice of many waters, and as the voice of a great thunder, which shall break down the mountains, and the valleys shall not be found.

"He shall command the great deep, and it shall be driven back into the north countries, and the islands shall become one land;

"And the land of Jerusalem and the land of Zion shall be turned back into their own place, and the earth shall be like as it was in the days before it was divided.

"And the Lord, even the Savior, shall stand in the midst of his people, and shall reign over all flesh." (D&C 133:1-25.)

The presence of the Jews in Palestine is physical evidence of the gathering of Israel in the last days. But there is another gathering of Israel also; that is, the gathering of the tribe of Ephraim. And who are they? New converts are joining the Church in many lands. Thousands of members have come to America, particularly to the area of the temples in the "tops of the mountains."

Patriarchs tell them, for the most part, that they are of Ephraim. They are as much of Israel as are the Jews. They are even more the covenant people than the Jews, for they have the same rights by birth as do the Jews. In addition, they have made their personal covenants with God through baptism, the sacrament of the Lord's Supper, the ordination to the priesthood, and the temple ordinances.

So two tribes of Israel are being gathered now, all in preparation for the coming of the Lord.

What of the ten tribes?

They, too, will be gathered in the Lord's own time. Says the prophecy concerning them:

"And they who are in the north countries shall come in remembrance before the Lord; and their prophets shall hear his voice, and shall no longer stay themselves; and they shall smite the rocks, and the ice shall flow down at their presence.

"And an highway shall be cast up in the midst of the great deep.

"Their enemies shall become a prey unto them.

"And in the barren deserts there shall come forth pools of living water; and the parched ground shall no longer be a thirsty land.

"And they shall bring forth their rich treasures unto the children of Ephraim, my servants.

"And the boundaries of the everlasting hills shall tremble at their presence.

"And there shall they fall down and be crowned with glory, even in Zion, by the hands of the servants of the Lord, even the children of Ephraim.

"And they shall be filled with songs of everlasting joy.

"Behold, this is the blessing of the everlasting God upon the tribes of Israel, and the richer blessing upon the head of Ephraim and his fellows.

"And they also of the tribe of Judah, after their pain shall be sanctified in holiness before the Lord, to dwell in his presence day and night, forever and ever." (D&C 133:26-35.)

It is remembered that Amos said, "Surely the Lord God will do nothing, but he revealeth his secret unto his servants the prophets."

Since God would not act without prophets, how could he accomplish the above eight great events which were to precede the Second Coming?

Most churches of the world do not believe in modern prophets, apostles, or revelation. Yet revelation from heaven is essential to the accomplishment of each of these events. What could the Lord do to bring about the fulfilment of all these prophecies pertaining to a preparation for the second coming of Christ when there was no prophet on the earth?

There was only one thing he could do—raise up a new one.

This he did, and that individual was the Prophet Joseph Smith who was an instrument in the hands of God for bringing to pass all eight of the preparatory events.

And with them, the Prophet also revealed sensible and full explanations of the many doctrines which have caused mankind to wonder.

He gave us the truth about death and immortality.

He gave us the truth about the Creation.

He brought back the spiritual gifts, now prominent in the Church as they were anciently.

He gave us a proper understanding of the Resurrection, both that of Christ and that to which we ourselves look forward.

He gave us an understanding of the eternal nature of the family, whereby each mortal family which complies with the gospel truths may remain intact through death and the Resurrection. He gave us eternal marriage to make this family life possible.

He gave us an understanding of the fatherhood of God and the brotherhood of man. We are the offspring, the actual children, of the Almighty.

He revealed to us our ultimate destiny—that we can become like our Father in Heaven and fulfil the command of Jesus to become perfect even as he and his Father are perfect. We not only can come back into their presence, but we can also grow to become like them and inherit the riches and opportunities of eternal advancement.

Like John the Baptist in his day, Joseph Smith in our day has truly laid the foundation for the coming of the Lord. He was that chosen messenger to go before the Lord. He prepared the way. He was the forerunner, and we who live today must carry the torch until the day when the Lord comes in glory, with all the holy angels—and the Saints and the prophets with him.

To see Joseph Smith in his true perspective as the forerunner of the Lord is to give us a better understanding of our own future and of the near approach of the millennial reign of Jesus Christ.

Index